PRAISE FOR *HOW TO GET PAID FOR WHAT YOU KNOW*

"Here's good news: you don't have to choose between growing a successful career and a fulfilling life. In *How to Get Paid for What You Know*, Graham Cochrane gives you a simple, actionable plan for creating an online business that gives you both. That's what I call the Double Win, and this book brings it one step closer!"

—Michael Hyatt, *Wall Street Journal* bestselling coauthor of *Win at Work & Succeed at Life.*

"You may not think it's possible to create an income and a life you love, but don't let what you think get in the way of what you want. In *How to Get Paid for What You Know*, Graham makes the case that now is the best time to create a business around what you know and love and gives you the step-by-step plan to do just that."

—Jon Acuff, New York Times bestselling author of *Soundtracks: The Surprising Solution to Overthinking*

"The two greatest financial levers imaginable are selling knowledge and creating residual income. If you understand those you will bypass the millions of hardworking people who are on what Graham refers to as the forty-year, nine-to-five grind. This book is the blueprint for what surely is the eighth wonder of the world."

—Dan Miller, author of *48 Days to the Work You Love*

"Brilliant, and much needed, this book can dramatically enhance your life and help you build a business and build a LIFE that is a lot more fun, a lot less stressful, and a lot more profitable...all while bringing immense value to those you serve. And what could be better than that!"

—Bob Burg, coauthor of *The Go-Giver* and Go-Giver book series

"Graham has massively over delivered value in this book. *How to Get Paid for What You Know* is worth at least 10 times what you'll pay for it. But not only is it valuable, it is delivered in an empathetic, life-giving way. If you're exhausted by many of the snake oil salesmen of the 'online business' world, you will find Graham's style refreshing. I wholeheartedly endorse this book from Graham Cochrane—the #1 person I trust when it comes to monetizing knowledge."

—Jordan Raynor, national bestselling author of
Redeeming Your Time: 7 Biblical Principles for Being
Purposeful, Present, and Wildly Productive

"Right now is the time to live the life of your dreams! Life is too short to continue putting off living the life that you feel most called to live. Graham is the real-deal in the digital entrepreneur space and in *How to Get Paid for What You Know*, he generously shares a proven and powerful system that will take your message, your business, and your life to the next level."

—Cliff Ravenscraft, Mindset & Life Transformation Coach

"As L.P. Jacks said, the master in the art of living makes no distinction between his labor and his leisure, a quote that has always been my life theme. In *How to Get Paid for What You Know*, Graham reveals a refreshingly simple strategy for creating an income online built around what you know and love. Watching his story unfold, and seeing his results up close, I love how he pursues life and business and after reading this I know you'll be both inspired and equipped to do the same."

—Jonathan "JCron" Cronstedt, President of Kajabi

"I love this book! I'm convinced it will be a huge help to so many people. And I am one of them. Graham has had such a huge impact in my life by shaping how I think about running my business. I am finding myself constantly going back to the principles he shares in *How to Get Paid for What You Know* to help me stay focused on achieving my goal of impacting people with my message."

—ill Factor, Grammy Nominated Producer and Founder of Beat Academy

HOW TO
GET PAID
FOR WHAT
YOU KNOW

HOW TO GET PAID FOR WHAT YOU KNOW

Turning Your Knowledge, Passion, and Experience
into an Online Income Stream in Your Spare Time

Graham Cochrane

Matt Holt Books
An Imprint of BenBella Books, Inc.
Dallas, TX

How to Get Paid for What You Know copyright © 2022 by Graham Cochrane

Published in association with the literary agency of Legacy, LLC, 501 N. Orlando Avenue, Suite #313-348, Winter Park, FL 32789.

BenBella Books, Inc.
10440 N. Central Expressway
Suite 800
Dallas, TX 75231
benbellabooks.com
Send feedback to feedback@benbellabooks.com

BenBella is a federally registered trademark.
Matt Holt and logo are trademarks of BenBella Books.

Printed in the United States of America
10 9 8 7 6 5 4 3 2 1

Library of Congress Control Number: 2021042847
ISBN 9781637740675
eISBN 9781637740682

Editing by Katie Dickman
Proofreading by Lisa Story and Michael Fedison
Indexing by Amy Murphy
Text design and composition by Aaron Edmiston
Cover design by Brigid Pearson
Cover image © Shutterstock/Nattalia Gubanova
Printed by Lake Book Manufacturing

To my daughters, Chloe and Vera. One of the greatest gifts of an online business is the freedom to spend so much time with you, watching you grow into amazing young women.

CONTENTS

INTRODUCTION

You are sitting on a gold mine.

Whether you realize it or not, you *already* have the knowledge, passion, and skills to create an automated income stream that requires no college degree, zero employees, and less than fifty dollars to get started.

Imagine with me for a moment. If you had an extra $1,000 or $5,000 coming in each month, what would that mean in your life? Alternatively, if your work only required twenty hours per week to generate a full-time income, how would your life improve?

Would you pay off some student loan or credit card debt? Would you take your kids to school every morning, work only half days, and then hang out with your family every afternoon and evening without needing to check your phone or email?

Or maybe you would give more money to your church while also having time to volunteer as well. Or perhaps you would go live in another country for a month and only check your laptop for two hours a week like I did with my family a few summers ago.

Sound impossible? Hardly.

It's becoming increasingly possible for more people to transition out of work that's not a good fit and into creative, fulfilling, and lucrative self-employment online.

MEANINGFUL, FLEXIBLE, AND LUCRATIVE WORK

Are you looking for a career change? Are you searching for meaningful work that both pays well and helps you sleep well at night knowing you're making a difference in the world?

Do you need a more flexible way to earn a living so you can take off whenever you like and have more control over your schedule?

If so, keep reading. You, my friend, are living in the most incredible time in the history of earning an income.

The ability to create an income around your knowledge, passion, and experience has never been easier. We are only at the beginning of a huge economic wave, and it's a great opportunity for nontraditional entrepreneurs to jump into the marketplace, add value, and change their lives.

How do I know? Because that is *precisely* my story. I was a musician living on food stamps who turned an obscure knowledge about recording music into a million-dollar-per-year business that requires just a few hours of my time each week.

FROM FOOD STAMPS TO FREEDOM

I know how it feels to dread Monday morning, to feel out of place and unfit for the forty-year, nine-to-five grind that is literally killing people. I've worked in retail, restaurants, and corporate America—and I never felt like I belonged. All the while, I believed *I* was the problem.

My passion for music seemed like just that, a passion, and nothing more. But in 2009, during the Great Recession, and in the aftermath of not one but two job losses, I made a seemingly insignificant decision that forever changed my life: I started a blog about music recording.

That blog turned into a YouTube channel and ultimately into a business that has helped me not only set my family up for life financially but also have all the time in the world to spend with those I love, doing what I love.

Not only did I fall in love with my newfound freedom, but also I fell in love with the business model that has created that freedom. And so over the last few years, I've begun sharing my exact formula for transitioning from nine-to-five jobs to online income streams, helping thousands of people each week do just that on my podcast, *The Graham Cochrane Show*, and through videos on my YouTube channel.

Now I want to share that exact same formula with you in this book.

JUST FOLLOW MY PROVEN SIX-STEP PROCESS

In this book, I'll show you exactly what I've done to build not one but two successful online businesses by introducing you to the dynamics of the knowledge economy and breaking down the six steps you can follow to excavate the gold mine that's right under your nose.

In the pages that follow, I will walk you through a step-by-step process for creating an income stream built on your knowledge, passion, and skills. These steps include:

- discovering your idea and ensuring it will be profitable;
- building an audience of loyal fans;
- packaging your knowledge into a highly desirable digital product;
- selling online in an authentic and ethical way;
- leveraging simple online tools to market your product; and
- automating the entire process so that income flows to you even when you're not working.

I will also address and answer common pressing questions such as the following:

- Why would people pay for information when there is plenty of information out there for free?
- How do I convince people to pay me for my knowledge if I don't feel like an expert and don't have impressive credentials?
- How do I build an income stream if I'm already busy with family, work, and life?

By the end of this book, you will not only know the exact step-by-step process for creating the income and life of your dreams, but also, perhaps more importantly, you will feel empowered to actually go and do it. Knowledge is one thing, but belief that turns into action is something else entirely. And action is where life change happens.

You can change your life if you apply what you read in this book. Even if you only have thirty minutes a day to work on your online business, you can create an income stream of $1,000, $5,000, or even $10,000 a month. It's not just possible for someone "out there," but for *you*! You can do this, and I'm here to coach you every step of the way.

Are you ready to change your life? Then let's begin.

Chapter 1

KNOWLEDGE COMMERCE

Why People Will Pay for What You Know

I never wanted to be an entrepreneur.

Growing up, I didn't know a single business owner or self-employed person, and my parents had "normal" nine-to-five jobs (my mom was a schoolteacher, and my dad was an engineer). I think part of the reason I never considered going into business was because of my narrow view of what entrepreneurship was.

When *you* think of business, what comes to mind?

Some tech genius from Silicon Valley inventing the next iPhone or Instagram? Or perhaps some brilliant young Harvard MBA student who aims to work herself up to CEO of a Fortune 500 company? Or maybe you simply think of your favorite local sushi restaurant. That's how I used to think about business. And to be honest, none of that appealed to me.

But neither did working a normal nine-to-five job like my parents.

I wanted something different. For me, it all started with music. When I was young, I had my sights set on being a rock star. Making albums in the studio, creating music videos for MTV (showing my age!), and touring the world as a famous singer/songwriter was all I ever wanted. I viewed myself as a creative—as an artist—and the idea of working a j-o-b or running a business seemed boring, stale, and simply not in my DNA.

But after a few years of chasing the music dream hard and not landing a record deal, I had to "grow up" and get a "real job."

My soul was crushed. I felt out of place wearing a shirt and tie and sitting in a cubicle every day, and I wondered constantly what people like me were supposed to do to make a living and not resent each and every moment of it. Then something crazy happened that altered the course of my life forever: the Great Recession of the late 2000s.

A BAD ECONOMY CHANGED MY LIFE

In 2009, at the age of twenty-six, I lost not one but *two* jobs in a single year, both thanks to the massive global recession.

In January of that year, I was informed that my department at the tech company I worked for was being dissolved. We got a tiny severance package and the day off. Yay! Later that fall, my wife and I moved to Tampa, Florida, to help a friend start a church. I landed a job, bought my first house, and my wife and I had our first baby. And then, just when things seemed to be looking up, my employer closed its doors. I was unemployed again.

So there I was in my midtwenties with a family, a mortgage, and a life in a new and unfamiliar place with no job, few prospects, and absolutely zero vision for my future. I felt like a total failure. I was scared, frustrated, and embarrassed.

After burning through what savings we had, my wife and I turned to freelancing, as we both at least had skills that were marketable. My wife is a photographer, and I had been a music producer on the side for years.

But it's hard to get work when you don't know anyone locally. In order to survive, we turned to the generous support of family and friends, and were even on food stamps for eighteen months to help pay for groceries.

I was at the lowest point of my life.

I knew I needed to do something to get more clients and try to make my freelance side gig a full-time income stream. So I did something that at the time seemed like an insignificant decision: I started a blog.

The Accidental YouTuber

The idea seemed simple: nobody in Tampa knew who I was, so in order to get more remote clients, I figured I might as well put myself out there on the internet, share what I'm doing in my home recording studio, and hope that people in need of music production help find me and hire me. I didn't know if it would work, but I certainly had a better chance of being found if I put something out there than if I didn't.

Little did I know, this single decision to create an online presence would become the foundation of a powerful business model I was about to discover, representing a seismic shift in my career.

The blog led to a YouTube channel in January 2010 where I began sharing screen recordings of what I was doing in my recording software. I renamed my blog and channel "The Recording Revolution" because I felt it described what I was excited about as a musician and producer—highlighting how recording equipment was becoming cheaper, more accessible, and relatively easier to use. The YouTube channel would become fuel for a larger fire that was beginning to burn.

Remember: my hope was that people would somehow discover my content, see that I was a competent audio engineer, and then ask to work with me.

Something else happened entirely. The people who were finding my videos and articles wanted more of them. They didn't want *me* as much as they wanted the knowledge I was sharing. While this was flattering, and I was glad to be helping some musicians figure out the art of recording their music at home, I still needed to make money. And fast!

If freelance production work wasn't the way to get there, I wondered if perhaps monetizing my content was. But how?

HOW DO BLOGGERS AND YOUTUBERS MAKE MONEY?

I'll be honest: it feels good to put a piece of content—an article, video, or podcast—out into the world and see people get something positive from it. The likes and comments are super encouraging.

But likes weren't putting food on my table. I couldn't keep spending time writing blog posts and shooting video tutorials if I couldn't pay the bills from it.

I was creating content people loved. Now, my mission was simple: find a way to monetize this content. I tried running ads on my YouTube videos, but that hardly paid anything without hundreds of thousands of views per month. I tried banner ads and sponsorships on my blog with brands that I knew would be a perfect fit for my audience. And that kind of worked. I think I made a few hundred dollars per month that way. But it became clear that, in order to make any real money, I would need something more profitable than ads. I would need my own products.

It dawned on me that if people really liked my video tutorials, they might actually pay me for a much longer, more in-depth, on-demand video course. I didn't have any proof of that concept at the time and didn't know if it was truly possible, but I had a feeling it might work.

My First Sale of My First Product

I spent about a week filming three to four hours' worth of videos covering a popular type of software used in recording studios. It was a comprehensive tutorial for working in this platform, taught in a way that was approachable and easy to understand.

I basically did what I'd done with my music friends countless times before when they came over for coffee and we sat down in my studio where I would show them this software. My goal was for them to leave feeling empowered and familiar with the ins and outs of the program so they could focus on what they really wanted to do—make music.

I threw all the video recordings up on my website server in a zipped folder and created a simple product page outlining what the videos were about and why I thought they would be super helpful. I didn't know anything about sales copy or marketing, but I did my best to articulate that I was offering something valuable and worth paying for.

That first product sales page was pretty ugly, by the way. I duct-taped it together with some free website software and added some PayPal buttons. But it was all I knew how to do. I sent a message out to my small email list at the time (more on email lists in chapter 5), traveled to Seattle to visit my grandparents, and afterward found myself in a café looking for Wi-Fi so I could check my email.

I opened my inbox, and there, on April 23, 2010, someone had sent me forty-five dollars via PayPal and downloaded my course. I had made my first sale of my first digital product! His name was Paul, and he was my first customer.

I knew it was just forty-five dollars, but it felt like so much more. It was proof of concept. If I could sell this course to one guy, what would happen if I sold this course to *more* people? And what if I made *more* courses to sell to those people? And what if I made *more expensive* courses and sold them? That forty-five-dollar sale way back in 2010 has now turned into an online business that generates over a million dollars in revenue each year and has spawned a second online business teaching people like you how to do the same.

But rest assured, I'm no fluke. As I soon discovered, there's *an entire industry* built around selling obscure knowledge like mine. On that April day back in 2010, I discovered what has come to be known as knowledge commerce, and I've never looked back.

KNOWLEDGE COMMERCE— A $243 BILLION INDUSTRY

At the time, I didn't know there was a term for what I was doing—selling information and knowledge online and building a business around it. It has many names, in fact, but my favorite is *knowledge commerce*.

The CEO of Kajabi (my favorite tool for running my online businesses), Jonathan Cronstedt, defines knowledge commerce this way:

When we use the term knowledge commerce, *we're referring to the practice of charging customers for access to our knowledge. This could be through an online course, an e-book, a membership site, or any other digital product designed to share knowledge.*

You might have heard this industry called online learning, e-learning, or some other name. We discovered, however, that none of those names sufficiently describe the industry we're talking about.

In school, teachers and professors are paid to share their knowledge in the classroom. The money comes from tuition, taxes, or some other source, and students meet in a physical classroom in a specific geographical area.

You might have noticed that many universities and colleges now offer what they call distance education. Students can get their degrees by participating in online lectures and submitting their projects via the internet.

But traditional teachers and professors aren't the only people who can spread knowledge in a commercial way. In fact, we believe that everyone has valuable knowledge that he or she can share with the world via knowledge commerce.

Consequently, we define knowledge commerce as any commercial enterprise that exchanges knowledge for cash.

According to Kajabi's research, knowledge commerce was a $243 billion industry in 2017, and some predict it will grow to a $331 billion industry by 2025. And these market trends existed prior to the COVID-19 pandemic, which has forced even more people online in search of information to start new careers or get better equipped for their current ones.

Here's what I've discovered: the knowledge-commerce industry is perfect for the non-business person who wants the benefits of a business without all the fuss. What I have built and what I will teach you how to build in this book could be called an online business, or an information product business, or an e-learning business, but I prefer to simply call it a knowledge-income stream.

Because that is exactly what it is—an income stream that flows to you each and every day that's built around your knowledge, skills, and experience.

NINE REASONS A KNOWLEDGE-INCOME STREAM IS FOR YOU

While there are many reasons to start a knowledge-income stream, I would like to highlight nine of my favorites.

1. **Low Cost to Start**
   The average cost to start a knowledge-income stream is only a few hundred dollars. In fact, I started my first, the Recording Revolution, with just fifty dollars. You don't need a custom website, money for advertising, or any other traditional start-up costs. And you certainly don't need to raise venture capital or get investors. If you can skip a meal or two in a restaurant with your family one month, you can have enough cash to get your income stream up and running.

2. **Low Friction to Start**
   Unlike many businesses, there is little to no friction to get started. You simply start a website, begin sharing content, build your audience, and then offer your paid digital products. You don't need permission to get started. You don't need a ton of planning. You don't even need to incorporate or get an LLC. You can start this weekend if you like. To be honest, the only real friction to getting started is your own fear and insecurity (more on that in a minute).

3. **Low Overhead**
   Much like a family budget, the key to making money and building wealth in a business is to watch your expenses. The

lower your overhead (i.e., monthly operating expenses), the more profit you get to keep. And this is one area where a knowledge-income stream shines—the ongoing costs to keep the doors open are minimal.

At its most basic, you simply pay for your website hosting. Most of the other tools are free or inexpensive. Even if you get a bit fancier and use an all-in-one platform like Kajabi (more on this tool in chapter 6), you're still spending less than $200 a month to create a six-figure (or more) annual income.

4. **No Employees Needed**
   If you're like me, you don't want to manage a team. You prefer to work for yourself and by yourself. If that's the case, you're in luck. The type of business I'm going to show you how to build virtually runs itself. The marketing, prospecting, sales, product delivery, and analytics departments are all handled by software, and that keeps your costs low and erases the need for personnel management. If you want to build a small team you certainly can, but they don't even need to be full-time employees. They can be part-time, independent contractors who all work remotely.

5. **High Profit Margins**
   Information products like online courses and membership sites have some of the highest profit margins of anything out there. The cost to build them is generally nothing but your time, and the cost to market, sell, and distribute is zero dollars because it's all baked into your normal monthly costs. What this means is that your products are virtually 100 percent profit. That's unheard of in business.

6. **Scalable Income**
   One of the best things about a knowledge-income stream is that your workload is pretty much fixed (and usually decreasing over time as you become more efficient and automate things—more on this in chapter 8). But your income potential is not tied to

your work. It's completely independent and quite scalable. As the years go on, you will get disproportionate results for the amount of effort you put in each week.

For example, I went from working thirty-plus hours a week on my income stream and making a few hundred dollars a month, to working only three hours a week and bringing in seven figures a year.

7. **Work from Anywhere**

With a knowledge-income stream, all you need is your laptop and an internet connection, and you are rolling! You can work from home and kill your morning/evening commute. You can work at a coffee shop and smell espresso all day long. Or you can rent a cool coworking space in your city and completely control your hours. You can even move to a different city or the other side of the world if you like. It doesn't matter where you are, because your work is online.

8. **Ultimate Flexibility**

When you set things up the way I'm going to teach you, your income is not determined by when or how much you work. What this means practically is you can dip in and out of work whenever it is convenient for you.

Are you a morning person? Then wake up early, get a few hours of work in, and be done by lunch. Are you a night owl? Then sleep in late, go for a run or walk, and start your day at 1:00 p.m. if you like. Don't feel like working this Monday? Take the week off and watch every single *Star Wars* movie instead. Or you can do what I did with my family a few summers ago—take six weeks off work and travel to the South of France where you can eat cheese and sip rosé all day!

9. **Do Work You Believe In**

And finally, one of the biggest benefits to starting a knowledge-income stream is one that I find many of my students craving:

the ability to do work that matters. I've worked in corporate America. I've felt like a square peg in a round hole. Like I don't belong and don't really care about the mission and vision of the company I work for; I'm just there for the paycheck. To me, that's a sad existence, and one I never wanted (remember my rock star dream?).

Building your own knowledge-income stream around what you know, love, and are good at gives you such a sense of purpose. You get to create things that excite you and help others. And when you are doing work that you believe in, you work harder and do it better. This of course leads to more success, which leads to more encouragement to keep doing more. It's a beautiful cycle that gets you excited to wake up in the morning and go serve more people.

HAVING SOME DOUBTS?

Now, that all might sound wonderful to you. But if you are anything like me when I got started, you're likely *very* skeptical that this dream can become a reality. Not skeptical that this has worked for me or others, but skeptical that it's possible for *you.*

And that's all that really matters at the end of the day, right? That this income model is possible for *you.*

I tend to see three common objections or doubts creep up when someone begins a knowledge-income-stream journey. If you can identify with any or all of these doubts, welcome to the club. That just shows that you're intelligent and you don't want to waste your time on something that ultimately will fail.

I like how you think.

Doubt #1—Why would people pay for my online course or membership site when there is plenty of information out there for free?

This is probably the number one question I get from students. And it's a logical one given how much helpful information is out there for free, located with just a single Google search. It becomes an even bigger question when you start to regularly give away a ton of your *own* great content for free (more on this in chapter 4). You might worry that your own free stuff is competing with your paid stuff. But that's simply not true.

You must understand that you aren't actually selling information—you are selling *transformation*. People don't go shopping for knowledge; they go shopping for results. People want change in their lives. Whether that change is weight loss, new or better relationships, a more profitable business, or better-sounding music—the desire is the same: improvement.

Information is only a means to an end. Never forget that.

So if what people are truly willing to pay for is results—transformation —then allow me to give you three reasons why, in a sea of ever-growing free online content, people will be happy to pay you handsomely for your premium digital products:

1. **People Are Overwhelmed with Content.** There's simply so much of it these days that it can be almost unhelpful. I always say: *Where there is overwhelm, there is opportunity.*

    Have you ever done a Google or YouTube search looking for a simple answer to a question only to find an hour of your life gone in what seems like seconds and so much conflicting information that your head is left spinning and you actually feel dumber after having done some research? Yeah, been there, got the T-shirt. Where the internet used to be fun and exciting, nowadays it can become overwhelming very quickly.

    That's where your online course or membership site comes in. You can curate all your best information into one convenient, easy-to-follow, step-by-step plan that gets your students from where they are to where they want to be with the least fuss possible.

2. **When It Costs Money, People Take It More Seriously.** Imagine you get some concert tickets to a great band for free from a friend. As excited as you are to go to that show, if something comes up that conflicts with the performance, you are more likely to skip the concert because it didn't cost you anything. But you better believe if *you* had paid for those tickets, you would have made sure you were there.

Or think about why people pay for personal trainers when they can work out at their gym without one for far less or just exercise for free at home. It's because spending money makes them accountable for taking action and getting results.

People really only value what they pay for. And that basic truth applies to information as well. Whether the material is better or not, people take an online course they paid for far more seriously than a simple YouTube video or blog post they found.

3. **People Are Getting More Than Information. They Are Getting Access.** When someone purchases your online course, they're getting more than just the great video content you will provide—they're getting access to you, the content creator. Public comments on a blog post or video can grow to be too many, prohibiting you from interacting with all of them and doing so thoughtfully. When a free student becomes a paid student, it is much easier for you to give them attention in the comments or community portion of your digital products (don't worry if this sounds like a lot of work; it's not, and I'll show you how I do it in a scalable way).

The fact that I'm offering not just my best content but also access to me directly is something that I present very clearly when selling my digital products. I will be their guide and coach, even if in a limited way, and my support will help them achieve their goals faster.

Doubt #2—Who am I to teach this? I'm not an expert. I don't have any credentials.

Man, this one is heavy. I struggled for years (and sometimes still do) to feel like I was credible enough to teach music recording on the internet, whether free or paid. While I *had* gone to school for audio engineering, I didn't feel like an expert. And I didn't have any big-name musicians as clients or a Grammy award to brag about.

Turns out there's a term for this feeling: impostor syndrome.

According to an *International Journal of Behavioral Science* article titled "The Imposter Phenomenon," 70 percent of people have feelings of being an impostor, or a fraud, in their work or career. Even highly educated and accomplished professionals like physicians and marketing executives deal with this. Successful or not, the fear is real for many of us.

When I started, I felt like an impostor with every video or article I put out. Like eventually someone would find out that I'm nobody special. That I'm just a guy who likes recording music and wants to share what I know with others. First off, you have to understand that this feeling is totally normal and might not ever go away. You're not silly for feeling unqualified. All that feeling proves is that you're human.

But there are two things you must remember about this knowledge-income-stream thing:

1. **People don't need you to be an expert—they need you to get them results.** At the end of the day, getting results for your students *is* your credibility. And by putting amazing free content out there in the world and letting people "test drive" your knowledge, they can see for themselves just how helpful you are.

    While having certifications or fancy letters at the end of your name is impressive, it really only is a means to bolster your own ego. *You* would feel better about yourself if you had a bunch of credentials. Your students don't care. They want help, and they want to see results.

2. **You just need to be one step ahead of them on the journey.** The people who will become your customers are those who you can help. And you can only help those who are just a few steps (or a lot of steps) behind you in their transformational journey. This means that you don't need to help everyone, just those whom you can. Don't look *up* at those who are ahead of you—look back at those whom you can help pull up alongside you and teach them everything you know.

As you grow in your own skill and experience, you will have even more to teach and share, and your pool of potential customers will grow as well. That's certainly been the case for me.

Doubt #3—I have no idea what I could teach or build a knowledge-income stream around.

Most people either have many interests, or they undervalue their own knowledge in an area that feels unimpressive to them, making it difficult to identify what knowledge they could offer others. In chapter 3, I will walk you through a simple process you can follow to discover your own profitable idea, but for now I need you to understand something that I wholeheartedly believe. **Every single person on this planet has something valuable to share with the world.**

You may not think so. And you might not see it in yourself yet. But that's OK. My job is to help you uncover that hidden value deep inside and show you how to turn it into a profitable income stream. So be patient.

PULLING THE CURTAIN BACK ON THE PERFECT INCOME MODEL

In the next chapter, I'm going to share with you my exact income model—the one I teach to all of my students. It's based around something I call the value circle—this idea that business isn't about taking, but rather about giving.

You'll also learn three critical truths about this type of income stream and why I'm willing to bet that if you build one yourself, you'll see success.

For now, though, I want you to take some action. At the end of each chapter, I will provide a simple Action Step to help you process what you've read and move you a little closer to your goal of building a profitable knowledge-income stream.

Here is your first Action Step:

If you knew it would succeed and you couldn't fail, what would having a profitable online business do for you and how would it improve your quality of life?

Write your answer down (even on your phone) and be as specific as you can.

Chapter 2

THE VALUE CIRCLE

The More You Give, the More You Earn

If you were to ask a hundred different people what the key to a successful business was, you would likely get several different answers. Answers like good leadership, bold vision, or great products. And those would be correct—to a certain point. In reality, there's something deeper than those, and simpler too.

There's a unique combination of ingredients that makes businesses successful, and it can seem impossible to pinpoint or replicate from the outside looking in. But it's there, and it's critical that you understand it.

Without your own "secret sauce" as the core driving principle of your income stream, you could have all the best tactics and tools in the world and still not make a dime. You could have all the best products in the world and not generate a sustainable income.

My entire income model (the one I'm teaching you in this book) is built around this principle. And the good news is it's incredibly easy to understand. In fact, it's so simple that I could draw it up on a napkin, and you would get it right away.

So what's the secret? Giving. Specifically, giving immense value at every touch point of your business.

But I'm getting ahead of myself. Before we talk about what good business *is,* we need to expose what it *is not.*

If I were to poll my audience and ask what they most wanted to learn about, the answer would likely have to do with sales and marketing strategies. The theory is this: the more I know about marketing, the more money I will make. But that simply highlights one of the biggest myths in business.

Myth: Business is all about using the right marketing and sales tactics.

Truth: Business is all about adding value to the customer.

Sound underwhelming or overly simplistic? Let's break it down with some simple logic.

Imagine for a moment that you run a business that has a slick website with perfectly researched pricing for your product, but that product is mediocre. How many sales do you think you will generate? Very few. Why is this? Because eventually, the people who were fooled into buying your crappy product will realize that it is just that—crap—and then they will tell the world on social media, and it's game over.

Now imagine you have a different business that has an ugly website and your pricing is a little off (maybe too high, maybe too low), but your product is super valuable and helpful. How many sales do you think you will generate? A lot—eventually. Why is that? Because even if it takes a while for people to give you a chance, once word gets out that your product is valuable, it's game over in a good way! You'll be selling those things like hotcakes.

What's the difference in these two hypothetical examples? Not the right website. Not the right marketing strategy. But rather a valuable product. But sales success doesn't start with a valuable product. Even if you have a great product/service, no one will buy from you if you don't first add value in other ways before the sale. Otherwise, how would they hear about you?

And once people *do* buy from you, they won't buy from you again if you don't add even more value after the sale. You see, at the beginning, middle, and end of a business transaction, adding value is the core component, the secret sauce, that *must* be present in order to make people feel really good about handing you their hard-earned money.

MORE BLESSED TO GIVE THAN TO RECEIVE

Another way to think about adding value to someone's life is to simply seek to serve them. And all serving is, at the end of the day, is giving. When you give, you are serving—you are adding value. These words are all synonymous in my book and equally vital to building a successful knowledge-income stream. Jesus of Nazareth said two thousand years ago, "It is more blessed to give than to receive," and I couldn't think of a better income model than that—to focus on giving more than you focus on receiving.

A more modern take on things comes from Bob Burg and John David Mann in one of my all-time favorite books, *The Go-Giver*:

> *All the great fortunes in the world have been created by men and women who had a greater passion for what they were giving—their product, service, or idea—than for what they were getting.*

But what does this focus on giving rather than getting look like in practice, and how does it apply to your knowledge-income stream? It's time to take out that napkin I alluded to earlier.

My Business on the Back of a Napkin

Imagine you and I are sitting at a bar (or café or a donut shop—I'm good with all three), and we're having a great time talking about life and business. You ask me: "Graham, I'd like to start a business, but it all seems overly complicated to me. Can you explain to me a simple business model that I can start, even if I don't have an MBA or a clue as to what I could offer the world?"

My eyes light up like my kids' on Christmas morning, and with a goofy smile, I whip out a napkin and a pen and proceed to draw a circle.

At the top of the circle, I write the word *Give* and draw an arrow that curves to the right along the circle to the three o'clock position (that's the right side of the circle in case you weren't a fighter pilot in the Air Force). On the right side of the circle, I write the word *Sell* and then draw an arrow following the circle to its bottom (or six o'clock), where I write the word *Overdeliver*.

From there, I draw an arrow that curves up and to the left side of the circle where I write the word *Receive*. Then I draw one final arrow that curves up to the top of the circle where we started with the word *Give*. And smack-dab in the middle of that circle, I write in all capital letters one simple word: *VALUE*. The napkin would look like this.

THE VALUE CIRCLE

This imaginary napkin drawing is what I call the value circle, and it's the essence of a knowledge-income stream. If you're familiar with Jim Collins's flywheel concept, then this will feel familiar. If not, don't worry. It's incredibly simple.

The value circle is made up of four elements—three that you give and one that you receive. Each element centers on the concept of value. And all four work together in an ongoing cyclical fashion, with each element affecting the others in a beautiful circle of awesomeness.

Here's how this all works in real life.

Step 1—Give

It starts by giving something away for free. I know you want to sell your knowledge, not give it away, but stay with me here. Unless you and I commit to giving some of our best stuff away for free, we will never get the opportunity to sell our paid products and make a good living.

Much like how free samples at Costco or a fourteen-day free trial of Netflix hooks customers and eventually leads to sales, giving away some of your knowledge through free blog, video, or podcast content gives people a taste of the value you have to offer. Your free content gives people a test drive of your experience and teaching style, which helps you earn credibility before ever asking for their money.

Now, I think a lot of people understand that free content is important to a degree, but they tend to want to skip through this step as fast as possible in order to focus on building and selling products like online courses or membership sites. Or at best, they crank out some mediocre content that sounds like everything else we've ever heard.

Big mistake.

In order for this value wheel to spin, you must start at the top by constantly serving up amazing free content. It's what begins to create momentum and will lead to maximum revenue down the road. Don't worry: I'll teach you exactly how to create the best free content on the planet in chapter 4. For now, just understand that this is a critical first element of your income stream.

Step 2—Sell

If you give away valuable free content that people simply love, then you will have earned the right to pitch your products to them. The best part is that, by pitching products after having given away so much valuable content, selling becomes natural and your conversion rate (the percentage of people who buy what you offer) will increase tremendously.

And not only that, but I have found my paid students are actually *honored* to buy my products because they feel it's almost out of respect for how much I have given them already in my free content. In chapter 6, I'll walk you through my process for building your first online course or membership site and how to know it'll be something your people can't wait to buy.

Quick preview, though: you can't build a great paid product until you've seen which parts of your *free* content resonate with your audience.

Step 3—Overdeliver

You would think that making the sale would be the end of the process as it relates to you adding value to your customers, but this is where great businesses separate themselves from average ones. At this point, you've added value for free, then offered a valuable product, and now we want to go the extra mile and delight them with a valuable surprise. It's not enough to deliver the product; you want to deliver *more* than you promised. And, boy, is this fun!

Typically, I like to do this by including a bonus video module or extra training inside the online course they purchased that is super valuable and only enhances their experience with the product. And the great thing here is that it doesn't take much to overdeliver. It's more the surprise of it that delights your customer. It was something unexpected and generous. We experience so little genuine surprise these days that a little of it can go a long way to creating a powerful connection with your customers.

Now, so far in the circle, you have given value at three critical junctures: before, during, and after the sale. What comes next is the fun part.

Step 4—Receive

When you sell something, the most obvious value you could *receive* is money. The income you generate from your business is the value you deserve, and it's a truly wonderful thing. But there is another valuable currency you receive when you've followed the value circle well up to this point—referrals. In the product-based business, these are more commonly called testimonials or reviews.

We all know the power of reviews. Jump on Amazon right now and look for a new coffee maker to buy. Other than price, what do you look for? Ratings and reviews! We want to know two things: Have other people purchased this product before? And did it work for them?

If the answer to both of these questions is yes, then you are more likely to purchase the product. If not, then you will likely look elsewhere. The same is true for selling information products like online courses.

If you have a bunch of great testimonials from happy students who have gotten great results with your material, then you can leverage those words in sales pages and emails, which will help you sell more product. And when you sell more product, you receive more income.

And here's the cool part—the more income we earn, the more value we can offer our people for free (and paid) for years to come, because we can continue to make a good living and stay in business. The more income we receive, the more we can invest in ourselves and grow our own knowledge (like buying the book you're holding in your hand) or invest in our businesses by hiring help or using a more powerful tool or designing a more beautiful user experience for our products.

All of which helps us to serve and give more, which only helps us to receive and earn more. And the cycle continues.

THE LAW OF COMPENSATION

You'll see as we get deeper into the nuts and bolts of building your knowledge-income stream that I want you to build a system. A system that is finely tuned with every part working in harmony. When you build your income stream around the value circle and it's working, even if it's just spitting out $500 each month, the path to growing your income becomes obscenely simple: serve more people.

Let's go back to *The Go-Giver* for a moment and unpack one of the big principles in that book called the Law of Compensation, which states:

Your income is determined by how many people you serve and how well you serve them.

Said another way, **your compensation is directly proportional to how many lives you touch**.

Have you ever wondered why people doing noble work like schoolteachers or firefighters are paid so little compared to athletes and movie stars? For example, both math teachers and movie stars add value (education and entertainment are both valuable to our culture). But a high school math teacher might earn $40,000 a year whereas an A-list movie star might earn $40 million a year.

Are movie stars truly more valuable than math teachers? No. They both are just as valuable to society. You could argue that teachers are more valuable than actors, honestly.

The difference is how much impact they have.

The difference in pay is not just in how talented they are or how good they are at what they do, but rather how many lives they touch. Most schoolteachers touch the lives of thirty or more students per year. A major movie star touches the lives of millions.

The big takeaway here is simple: **If you want to increase your income, the good news is that it's under your control—just go serve more people.** And, according to Bob Burg, a powerful second (but potentially missed) takeaway is this: *"There are no limitations on what you can earn because you can always find more people to serve!"*

Do you see?

Creating a profitable and life-changing online business has little to do with tactics, manipulation, or luck. Rather, it has everything to do with finding as many people in your niche as possible and serving them well.

THE TRUTH ABOUT THIS TYPE OF INCOME STREAM

Hopefully by now, you're starting to see just how simple and exciting this type of giving-focused knowledge-income stream is. In the next section, we will begin the process of actually building *your* income stream. But before we get into the six-step process for building it, I need to tell you the truth. Three truths, to be specific.

Truth #1: This income model works—over time.

If you're looking for quick money, a knowledge-income stream is not for you. I don't believe in get-rich-quick schemes. I don't even believe in get-rich-relatively-soon schemes. Why? Because I've fallen for them in the past and been disappointed.

Years ago, when I was still wearing a shirt and tie and sitting in a cubicle, I spent most of my days not working but instead surfing the web looking for work-from-home opportunities. I know: I was a horrible employee. Don't judge me. Back then, I would find these websites that had a picture of a smug-looking guy standing in front of a bright-red Ferrari or a huge mansion and be sucked into the dream—the lifestyle that I wanted. Now, to be clear: I didn't want a Ferrari or a mansion (OK, maybe I wanted the mansion), but I wanted the *freedom* that this guy offered.

The ability to make good money, quickly and easily, was enticing. And so I fell for the bait and paid hundreds of dollars to get access to some "program" or "opportunity" to make a great living in just a few weeks or months.

In case you were wondering, none of that came true. At least not with those scams.

Instead, when I started my first business, the Recording Revolution, I worked diligently on my content, products, and customer service, and developed the business model I just outlined for you. I went from making a few hundred dollars a month in my first year, to earning about $1,000 per month in the first half of my second year, to earning $60,000 a year by the end of two years. And just a month later, I was earning $10,000 a month, and it just skyrocketed from there.

No, this model is not sexy. And some might call it slow. But if you do what I teach, it will work over time.

As billionaire investor Warren Buffett once said when asked why everyone doesn't copy his simple investment philosophy, it's "because no one wants to get rich slow."

For example, just the other day, I was having dinner with some buddies from my Bible study who are starting their own knowledge-income streams, and one of them said: *"Graham, I feel like I'm doing all this work, shooting these videos, sending out emails, building my audience, but I haven't made a dime yet."*

I then proceeded to tell him about the skyscraper that they're building next to my office in downtown Tampa. They'd been building that thing for months, and I'd seen literally zero progress from my window. Why? Because in order to build a tall structure that is strong and durable, you need to dig a deep foundation. And that takes time, with little impressive payoff.

But as soon as that foundation was done, the rest of the building has been going up super quickly. It's almost as if they turned up the speed ten times. That's what happens when you build this type of income stream. It's slow and steady for a while, but you're building a foundation that will last and can hold up a powerfully profitable business.

Truth #2: It doesn't matter if the idea has been done before—there's room for you and your unique voice.

We'll get into this more in the next chapter, but I feel the need to address it here before we go any further together. You might already have a clue as to what topic or niche you want to build your knowledge-income stream around, and you might be getting nervous if you look around and see that your area of interest is quite saturated and has many great voices at the helm.

Have no fear. None of those voices are *your* voice. Remember, it's not really about information as much as it is about transformation. And your unique personality and perspective will resonate with certain people more than other voices will. There are people out there right now who need your voice in order to see results in their lives.

Keep this in mind: Originality isn't the goal. Helping people get results is.

Truth # 3: You don't have to give up your entire life for this.

Finally, you might be the person who already feels overwhelmed in life, with family, work, and other responsibilities. So all this talk about creating content, building products, and adding value seems exhausting and slightly impossible. You want this income stream because you want freedom, not more stuff to do.

To you, I say: start small. Spend just thirty minutes a day if that's all you have right now. That adds up to about three hours a week (assuming you take one day off), which is ample time to start building your business. Don't be in a rush. Be realistic about how much time you can devote to this. The last thing I want is for you to burn out and quit.

And as you'll see in later chapters, making more money isn't directly tied to working more hours. I work less than I ever have in my life and make more than I ever dreamed possible. And it's not because I have employees doing everything for me. As we go down this road together and begin building your knowledge-income stream, I want you to keep in mind something that I have learned: your business should serve your life, not the other way around.

LET'S UNCOVER YOUR PROFITABLE IDEA!

In the next section of this book, I'm going to walk you through my six-step process for building, launching, and automating your online business, and we will start in the next chapter by discovering your profitable income idea.

I'll show you my three-part profitability framework for uncovering an idea that is virtually guaranteed to make money. That way you don't waste time building a website, a product, and a business that no one cares about.

Action Step:

Can you think of a business or brand that you feel embodies the value circle well? One in which generosity, surprise, and delight are at the core of what they do? Take a moment to write down how, from the customer's perspective, that business gives value before, during, and after the sale.

Chapter 3

STEP 1: FIND YOUR IDEA

The Three-Part Profitability Framework

I've heard it said that success leaves clues. The idea being that if you want to be successful you should pay attention to what successful people do.

Seems reasonable enough to me. So I try to pay attention not only to what successful business owners and CEOs do but also to what they *say* when it comes to growing a profitable business. And do you know what a lot of people tend to say?

Follow your passion!

Have you ever heard that one before? Uh-huh. Or what about its close cousin: *If you do what you love for a living, you'll never work a day in your life again.* Classic, inspirational stuff! I'm about 99 percent positive that both of those statements are shared, in some form or another, at every single high school and college graduation ceremony by a commencement speaker.

In 2016, TV personality Mike Rowe (most known as the host of the Discovery Channel's *Dirty Jobs*) said this, however, in a video commencement address for recent grads: "Don't follow your passion. When people follow their passions, they miss out on all kinds of opportunities they didn't even know existed."

He then went on to put it more bluntly: "Just because you're passionate about something doesn't mean you won't suck at it."

Yikes! My middle school guidance counselor never seemed to bring that up in our conversations.

What Rowe is getting at is super important for you and me to understand. If our goal is to create a profitable income stream, we have to be smart and do what it takes to provide enough value in the world that we are then compensated for it. If our passion doesn't add value for others, it won't pay.

Here's the dirty little secret: no one cares what business you want to start unless there's something in it for them! Just because I'm passionate about eating pizza doesn't mean people will pay me for it—unless I can find a way to add value to them in my pizza eating.

Just because I'm passionate about watching football (#GoBucs) doesn't mean I can follow that passion blindly and people will pay me to sit at home and watch football. (Sidenote: if I figure out how to actually monetize that passion, I will let you know and then proceed to hide out on my couch until Jesus calls me home!)

Sure, people may tell you to "follow your passion" if you want to be successful in business, but that's only half true. Your passion matters little if no one is willing to pay for it. Because unlike in the Kevin Costner film *Field of Dreams,* if you build it, they will (not) come. That's not how this works.

In this chapter, I want to teach you my three-part framework for filtering your passions and skills through the lens of what people will truly value in the marketplace. **That way you don't waste time building a website, product, and a business that no one cares about.**

Yes, I said *passions.* Because despite what we've just covered, passion is incredibly important. I'll toss it back to Mike Rowe to sum it up: "Never follow your passion, but always bring it with you."

STEP 1: START WITH WHAT YOU KNOW, LOVE, AND ARE GOOD AT

What I love about this type of business is that it works best when it is based around what you know, love, and are good at—three things you already are in possession of. You already have knowledge, skill, and passion for a topic (or topics) that makes you uniquely positioned to add value to others and build a highly profitable income stream.

I've never been a fan of owning a business that I don't personally care about. I've never wanted to own a restaurant, a dry cleaner, or a box subscription service. Certainly, those are appealing for some, but not me. Rather, I'd prefer to wake up each day and talk about something I truly believe in, care about, and have an intimate knowledge of. Especially if what I know can help improve someone's life, even by just 1 percent.

I know we just talked about how following your passion isn't rock-solid advice, and that what matters is building a business around what people actually are willing to pay for. We'll get to that in the next two steps. But for now we *must* start with what we love because I guarantee you: something you know and love can be turned into a business.

So, in this step, we get to be selfish. We get to start with what we love, know, and are good at, which quite honestly is fun. But this kind of self-reflection can actually be challenging for some people. Especially if they've been conditioned to simply work hard and forget about having a dream job or dream career.

To help you brainstorm some topics or niches to build your business around, I've come up with a simple list of four questions. What I'd like you to do is get a piece of paper (or Google Doc or Notes app) and simply write down whatever comes to mind as you ask yourself these questions. Don't judge yourself; just write down the answers.

Question 1: "What comes easy to me?"
What do you know about yourself that is supernatural for you? It may not seem all that special, but if you look around at friends, family, and the general population, this skill is something that doesn't come easy for everyone, but it does for you.

Question 2: "What do people say I'm good at?"
Other people have likely told you what your strengths are. Whether as a child growing up, or now as an adult, they've told you: "Oh, you're

so good at ____!" Notice any trends? In your circle of friends, church community, or family, what are you known for being good at?

Question 3: "What have I helped people do in the past?"

You've likely lent a helping hand to friends or family in a certain area. What is it? What is the thing (or things) that people tend to call or text you for help with? Are you handy with a saw and power tools? Do people ask you to help them with their finances? Have you found yourself giving relationship counsel to all your friends?

Question 4: "If I had a Saturday afternoon completely free, what would I spend hours reading about?"

Imagine this Saturday all your plans are canceled, your house is clean, and you have zero responsibilities for the day. If you plopped down in your chaise lounge (or leather recliner, if that's how you roll) and picked up a magazine, what would it be? What nonfiction books would you read? What blogs and YouTube channels would you scroll through? We tend to dive deep into topics we really are passionate about, so think about what topics you like to jump into headfirst when given some extra free time.

From your answers to these four questions, you should be able to come up with a list of five to ten topics or niche ideas that could be the foundation of your business. As you've been jotting them down, they are likely in no particular order, other than what came to mind. What I want you to do now is to reorder them from most interesting and exciting to you to least interesting and exciting.

Simply ask yourself, "Which of these top five or ten ideas gets me the most fired up?" and then do the same with the remaining ideas, all the way down to the last. You will have now prioritized your areas of knowledge, passion, and skill into the order that *you* prefer.

Finally, circle the top three ideas. These are the ones that you will focus on in the next two steps.

STEP 2: CUSTOMER RESEARCH 101

Now that we've had a moment to be selfish and think about what *we* would love to talk about all day long for a living, it's time to filter these top three ideas (or subject areas) through the lens of what real people find valuable. And the way we do this is through a process that most normal human beings despise: research.

I don't know about you, but I hated writing research papers growing up. The entire process was mind numbing to me. Doing the research, citing my sources, and somehow eloquently putting it all into a boring term paper just made me want to smash my head against a wall. Lucky for you, we aren't doing that kind of research here.

Instead, think of this step as treasure hunting. We have a hunch that there is buried treasure on this beach somewhere and, doggone it, we are going to find those golden nuggets! But instead of using a metal detector or shovel, our treasure hunting tools of choice are social media and email.

If you got a little nervous when I brought up social media, don't be. This step doesn't require you to have a large following on any platform. It technically doesn't require you to be on social media at all. All we are trying to do here is get some quick interactions with *real humans* to test out our ideas.

You can replace social media with friends and family. And that can be in person, online, or over text. The point is simply that we want to quickly get a pool of people's attention so we can ask them two simple but profound questions:

- "What is your biggest frustration related to _____ ?"
- "What is your biggest hope or dream related to _____ ?"

In case you were wondering, the blank is your initial topic or niche idea. And these two questions are really two sides of the same coin. The answers will tell us a lot about how much (or little) real people care about what you care about and, more specifically, what they need help with.

With the first question, you're trying to find out what pain points (if any) exist in the minds and hearts of real people when it comes to your idea. **Frustrations are problems waiting to be solved, and solving problems is what business is all about.**

For example, if I had listed healthy eating and nutrition as my number one passion during my brainstorming session, I would hop on Instagram or Facebook and ask my friends, family, and followers something along the lines of this:

"Hey there! I'm thinking about creating some helpful content on how to eat healthy and feel great, but I'm curious to know what you think about food. When it comes to healthy eating and nutrition, what is your biggest frustration? Just leave a comment below. I'll read every one. Thanks so much in advance."

The responses you get will be very telling, so write them down. People might answer in this hypothetical that they don't know what is truly good for them or not. All the nutrition science seems to be conflicting. Or they might say it's too expensive and time consuming to prepare healthy and nutritious meals for their family. Or perhaps their frustration lies in the fact that they don't like the taste of vegetables and they have a major sweet tooth.

Golden nuggets!

You should also ask the second question because not everyone thinks in terms of frustrations. Many people think aspirationally, envisioning what they hope to be a reality but isn't quite yet. **Realizing people's hopes and dreams is another surefire way to be in business for a long time.**

Keeping with our nutrition-and-healthy-eating example, we might email some friends and family and ask a variation of this question:

"Hey friend! As someone who is super passionate about healthy eating and nutrition, I'm trying to help as many people as I can achieve their goals in this area. And I need your help. When it comes to your body and your relationship with food, what is your biggest hope or dream for the next twelve to twenty-four months? Just reply to this email. It would mean the world to me."

You might get emails back that say things like: "I want to lose weight, and I know that what I'm eating is a huge factor in achieving that goal." Or, "I want to feel wide awake and full of energy every day without having to load up on coffee and sugar." Or perhaps they might say, "I've had a few people in my family drop dead of a heart attack in their fifties, and I just want to live a long healthy life."

More golden nuggets!

Whether on social media, via email or text, or in person, dialogue with people who respond and dig deeper when appropriate. You can always follow up with this simple line: "Thank you for sharing. That makes so much sense. If you don't mind me asking, can you tell me more about that?"

Throughout this process, jot down any and all interesting responses wherever you take notes. **Your goal here is twofold: (1) see if anyone cares, and (2) when they do, try and spot trends and take note.**

Now what do you do if after a few days and weeks of asking these two questions, you get crickets (i.e., no one responds)? Here are three quick suggestions:

- **Ask more specific questions.** You might need to lead people a bit more in this process. Sometimes, a lack of answers is due to a question that is too open-ended. So tee it up a little bit more for your people by asking something more direct, like: "Have you ever tried a diet only to fail in the first couple of weeks? How did you feel?" This pointed question is narrow in scope and appeals to emotions. Try a few different questions and see if they elicit more feedback.
- **Move on to another topic from your list.** If after zooming in tighter with your questions, people *still* aren't responding, you might need to change gears. Perhaps people just aren't interested in that topic or skill. If so, move on down the list that you made in step 1 and repeat step 2 related to that topic or niche.
- **Go back to the drawing board and brainstorm.** Absolute worst case, none of your ideas seem to connect with people. If this seems to be happening, you might need to dig a little deeper with your skills and passions and start the process over again.

Use the Talent Stack

Sometimes, one passion or skill isn't enough to build a business. In many cases, stacking them together can make all the difference.

Famous *Dilbert* cartoonist Scott Adams has this amazing concept he calls the talent stack. **The idea is simple: to be successful, you don't need to be the best at any one thing, but rather be great at a combination of things.** I'll let him explain.

> *The idea of a talent stack is that you can combine ordinary skills until you have enough of the right kind to be extraordinary. You don't have to be the best in the world at any one thing. All you need to succeed is to be good at a number of skills that fit well together. For example, I'm not much of an artist, not much of a business expert, and my writing skills are mostly self-taught. I'm funny, but not the funniest person in my town. The reason I can succeed without any world-class skills is that my talent stack is so well designed.*

This is one reason I believe the Recording Revolution was so successful. I'm a good audio engineer (but not amazing), I'm a solid songwriter (but not Grammy winning), and I'm a talented singer (though certainly not world class). But it was my combination of music creation and knowledge of audio recording and equipment that allowed me to bring people in to my studio virtually and show them how to create their own music cheaply and professionally—and that launched a business that changed my life.

So, if you're feeling stuck, get creative and implement the talent stack. Take your two or three (or more) talents and interests and stack them together into something new, then go out in the world to see if this combination is valuable to people.

STEP 3: CUSTOMER RESEARCH 201

At this point, you've done some really good stuff. You've gotten clarity on what knowledge, passions, and skills get you excited, and you've begun to discover if any of those line up with what real people find valuable or helpful.

But now we want to cast our net even wider to include the general public.

If this were an economics class, think of the last step as microeconomics (zooming in to what real individuals think and feel regarding your topic). This third and final step is more like macroeconomics, where we zoom *out* and look at big-picture trends with a larger sample size of the population.

If through this process you've been getting good feedback on your idea and want to dig even deeper, here are some other places to do research. Think of this as your 201 class.

There are two places I want you to do some digging: Amazon and Google.

When it comes to knowing if people care about your idea, all we have to do is see what (if any) books are being published on that topic or niche. Books contain information that, when applied, can lead to transformation, which ultimately is what people want and need in their lives. The mere existence of books in your niche indicates that someone (likely a major publisher) believes there is money to be made there. And assuming there *are* books on your topic, you can take advantage of a powerful resource: Amazon.com.

Leverage the Power of Amazon

Amazon is the world's leading online book retailer, which means if a book exists, it's likely for sale there. Plus, millions of people buy their books (both physical and electronic) on Amazon, so you're working with an insane amount of useful data. On top of that, Amazon gives you an even deeper insight into the minds of customers with its reviews feature. Here's a simple three-step process to leverage its power.

Find the top-five books in your topic or niche. Open up the Amazon app or navigate to Amazon.com in your favorite web browser and, under the books section, type in your topic or niche (e.g., "healthy eating" or "nutrition"). Ignore what books pop up initially. Re-sort the book results by Most Reviews, as this will pull up the likely best-selling books in that category. Now write down the top five books in that list.

Take note of their titles, subtitles, and tables of contents. The authors, editors, and publishers of these books have already done the work for you by figuring out what keywords, topics, and psychological positioning resonate with your niche's target market. So why not stand on the shoulders of giants? There is a feature called *Look Inside* that you can activate by simply clicking on the book image. Once opened, click on the table of contents link and write down the chapter names you see.

Read the two-, three-, and four-star reviews. You always want to ignore five-star and one-star reviews. These people are either fanboys or haters, and neither help you achieve your goal, which is honest feedback from average readers. What you're looking for in these reviews are two simple things: what people really liked about the book and what they felt was missing or off-putting. A book is a best seller for a reason, so you want to know why that is. But no book is perfect or completely addresses every issue at length, so you want to discover what gaps exist in the marketplace that you can fill.

This simple exercise is not only fun but also incredibly valuable because you can easily fill up your notebook or idea doc with a ton of real-world information that can help you in later steps of this process, such as content creation, product development, and writing compelling sales copy.

Now let's talk about one of your most powerful tools for researching for your business.

Google Knows All

Imagine there was a magical box that virtually every human on planet Earth with internet access could submit their deepest and darkest fears, questions, desires, and random musings to on a daily basis. And imagine if that box neatly organized and categorized those submissions by most submitted to least submitted. And imagine you could access those submissions yourself whenever you wanted, instantly, and at no cost.

Well, it *does* exist. Of course, I'm talking about the Google search bar.

Google.com is the number one visited website in the world every single day. It truly is the starting place for most people's internet journeys. But it's more than only that; it's the place where people share the truth about how they think and feel.

Google is the place you can safely and anonymously ask the questions you might be afraid to ask a friend. Or it's the place you go when you have a burning question that you need a quick answer to and you don't know who else to ask. And while you and I might casually use Google by typing some words in the search bar and then go about our days, all the while in the background, Google is remembering every single thing we type. Every. Single. Thing.

Kinda creepy, right?

Have you ever noticed that when you begin to type something in the search bar, Google begins auto-populating search suggestions based on what you first typed in? You might, for example, type in the words "how to lose weight," and Google tries to fill in the rest before you can hit another key stroke by throwing up some suggestions like "how to lose weight fast," or "how to lose weight in the face."

These auto-suggestions are literally what thousands, maybe millions, of other people have typed into Google. And they are words, phrases, or questions that Google thinks are relevant and often submitted. In essence, this is what people are thinking about and seeking answers for.

With that knowledge in mind, your task is simple: type your niche into Google and see what it auto-suggests.

Try it right now if you can. Referencing our earlier example, I just typed "healthy eating" into the Google search bar, and here's a list of suggestions that popped up:

- healthy-eating plan
- healthy-eating habits

- healthy-eating recipes
- healthy eating for kids
- healthy-eating tips
- healthy-eating quotes

What can we learn from these results? Lots. First, if no suggestions (or very few) pop up, then perhaps those keywords aren't very popular. Try to rephrase what your idea or topic is. Second, the details give us clues as to how we can focus our niche even more. Should we build a business around healthy eating for kids and target moms? Or should we focus on meal plans and recipes instead of the science and health studies? All interesting stuff.

Bonus tip: you can do the exact same thing on YouTube. Seeing as how YouTube.com is the second most visited website in the world (and owned by Google's parent company, Alphabet), it has just as powerful data capture available to you with the same search-bar auto-suggestions feature.

As with the Amazon book reviews, take note of what Google and You-Tube are telling you people care about and write it down in your master document. This step will either give you further clarity on your chosen niche, or it will cause you to pause and consider going back to the drawing board with a different topic. Either way, you're gaining valuable information for your business.

FIVE FINAL THOUGHTS ON THIS PROCESS

Before I leave you to the idea-validating process, let me give you five pieces of advice for navigating this process with even more success.

1. **Finding your profitable business idea will take time.** Deep customer research takes time and work. You can't discover your business idea in one afternoon. Commit to the process, and it will pay off. The last thing you want is to build a website, product, and platform around a topic that nobody cares about.
2. **Go deep with a few people one-on-one.** Most of this research can be done quickly and easily on the internet. And that's great.

But I highly suggest you be willing to make the effort to have a few in-depth conversations with people to probe deeper. Sometimes, the first answer to a question isn't the real answer. The good stuff is down a few layers, and those insights can prove to be invaluable as you build your business.

When I started researching for my online business-coaching brand, I asked people why they were interested in starting a business. I heard lots of answers, most related to wanting more money, time, and freedom. But when I dove deeper, I learned that many people had families and simply wanted the flexibility to take their kids to school and pick them up afterward without needing to be stuck in an office with a boss telling them what to do. That specific insight has been woven into my messaging since day one, and consequently, my brand resonates with men and women with families, which distinguishes me from many other online business "gurus."

3. **Look for trends and spot momentum.** If you notice lots of engagement on one type of post or one topic, perk up! Look for signs of intrigue and energy. Not every specific subtopic or question in your niche will be super popular. But a few will be. Look for those key pain points or dreams that keep coming up over and over again.

4. **You don't have to be original.** My first business (Recording Revolution) wasn't original. There were plenty of businesses teaching music recording and production when I started. I was still able to create a seven-figure income with it. In case you didn't know, I'm not the first person to dive into the business space either. Crazy, I know. That didn't stop me from turning my personal brand into a million-dollar-a-year business either. Remember: you're looking for what people find valuable, not unique.

5. **If lots of people are doing it, that can be good.** Don't buy into the "it's been done before" myth. If it's being done by lots of people, that means it's a valuable idea and there's a market for it. I'd much rather build a business where I know there is demand

for what I'm offering than jump into a space that has no buyers. But if you're feeling totally like a carbon copy of everyone else in your niche, remember the talent stack if you want to stand out.

IT'S TIME TO BUILD AN AUDIENCE

Well, friend, there's your three-part profitability framework. By brainstorming your knowledge, passions, and skills and filtering them through the lens of what real people—both those close to you and all over the world—find valuable, you will arrive at one, two, or maybe even three viable business ideas that you can be certain will turn a profit.

If you complete this process, you will be well on your way to building a business that people will engage with and buy from. **The sad reality is that most people want to skip this step and start posting to Instagram and packaging up an online course.** But eventually, they'll figure out that no one wants to buy what they're selling.

Not you. You're doing it right. You're starting with a strong foundation (research) that we will build upon in the next chapter by actually creating your most valuable asset: your audience. With that audience in place, you'll be able to sell anything and everything with confidence, knowing your superfans are waiting in line to buy from you.

Action Step:

Set aside three hours this weekend to work through the steps outlined in this chapter. Make it a goal to know within the next seven days which topic or niche you are going to build your business around.

Chapter 4

STEP 2: GROW YOUR AUDIENCE

How to Consistently Get Discovered Online with Content

Let me start this chapter by being honest with you about something: we're still two entire chapters away from beginning to talk about making money. That's right—you're reading a book about how to make money online that doesn't even start explaining how to make any money till half-way through. What am I, crazy?

Nope. I want you to make a lot of money. I'm a fan myself. And we *will* get to the product development, sales, and marketing steps soon, but in order to get there and be successful in business, I need you to understand something critical.

Without an audience, nothing is possible. But with an audience, *anything* is possible.

When people think about knowledge-commerce businesses, they think that having an online course or subscription product is the most important thing. In reality, the biggest asset you will ever have in business is your audience.

Yes, you will need a good online course (or two or ten), but if you don't have an audience of warm leads to sell that course to, you have nothing. A great course + warm audience = money. A great course + no audience = no money. It's the audience that makes the difference.

If you have an audience of superfans who love you and what you stand for, you actually don't even need an online course to make money. You could offer personalized coaching, a done-for-you service, or get paid to do brand deals as an influencer. The possibilities are endless—but only if you have an audience.

Great, but how does one build an audience?

The good news is that audience building (i.e., getting people's attention) is easier now than ever before.

When it comes to getting in front of people and building an audience, there is essentially one main method being touted today: paid ads (think Facebook ads, Google Adwords, or YouTube ads). And while the paid-ads route is often the tool of choice for many of my peers who teach others how to build knowledge-income streams, I run counter to that advice.

Not only do I not teach the paid-ads method (nor do I use them myself), I take things a step further and make fun of paid traffic like Facebook ads as a marketing strategy for online businesses. And for good reason: paid ads are, in my opinion, expensive, inefficient, and completely unnecessary for the type of business I'm teaching you how to build. I want to share with you a better strategy, one I've been using for more than a decade in two completely different niches, one that has helped me build *two* seven-figure businesses.

The secret to building a powerful audience and the method I prefer to use is called content marketing. What is content marketing? **Simply put, content marketing is the strategy of creating original, valuable, free content that your ideal customer wants to consume.**

Content can be written blog posts, YouTube videos, podcasts, or even social media posts. It can be education, entertainment, or even "behind the scenes" of your life. Anything that helps teach, inspire, motivate, or entertain your target audience can work.

The reason content marketing is called marketing is because it is a tool that helps you and your brand get discovered online. Much like an ad, your content brings awareness to your target market that you exist. When people search for things on Google, your blog posts can show up in the results. And as I'll share in a minute, it's not that hard to do. The same is true for your videos on YouTube. Your content goes out in the world *so that* it can be discovered organically when people are looking for it.

But how does content marketing actually compete with paid ads to attract your ideal future customer? Let me share with you not one, not two, but five ways content is king.

FIVE REASONS CONTENT MARKETING IS KING

1. **Content is free.** Creating content costs nothing but your time. Paid ads, well, cost money.

    Most of my students starting out have little money available to throw at ads so they prefer free methods. I make plenty of money these days but still prefer not to give any of it to Mark Zuckerberg and company at Facebook, so I stick with content marketing even now.

    In fact, one thing I've noticed is how many online business "gurus" will tout how much money their business makes in a launch or per month, but they never tell you how much of that went to ad spend. Last I checked, spending $20,000 to make $30,000 is worse than spending nothing to make $15,000.

2. **Content is evergreen.** One of the problems with paid ads is that they eventually go away (unless you keep paying for them). Content, on the other hand, lives forever.

    Much like an evergreen tree that never loses its leaves, your blog posts or videos may cost you time to create at first, but they live on forever on the internet, always working for you in the background. For example, every day, people discover my brand Recording Revolution because of a simple video I shot five years ago. How awesome is that?

3. **Content creates trust and credibility.** To put it bluntly, our eventual goal in online business is to make a sale. Otherwise, we don't eat. This means we need to create trust and rapport with our prospects before they decide to become customers. Building a product, throwing it up on a website, and either hoping random people will find it or running paid ads to promote it aren't great strategies.

    All of that is promoting to what we call cold traffic. You're basically selling to total strangers. We want to only sell to warm traffic, or people who already know, like, and trust us. By creating amazing free content that people can engage with first on their own, your audience gets a taste of what you have to offer, and they feel more comfortable buying from you.

4. **Content is shareable.** When you find an amazing article or video that helps you in a real and tangible way, you are inclined to share it. You might post it on social media or mention it in a private community you're a part of. If you're like my mom, you might even email it to everyone in the family.

    Good content not only gets discovered through search engines, it compels people to do the marketing *for* you and share it with others. Not many Facebook ads can say the same thing.

5. **Content is generous (and generosity is magnetic).** In a crowded sea of sponsored posts and paid ads, truly valuable free content stands out in the best way possible. When I create a piece of content for my brands, I try to give the goods. I don't hold back. Forget fluff; forget teaser pieces. I only deliver truly helpful and generous free content. People know value when they see it, and they are drawn to it like a magnet.

    Generous people are magnetic, and so are generous brands. When you find a YouTube channel or blog that answers all of your questions (for free), you can't help but love it. The same can be true of your content. Remember the value circle from chapter 2? The more you give, the more powerful your brand becomes.

Some people roll their eyes when I talk about content marketing. I get it. It's not nearly as sexy as cracking the Facebook ad code. But it works. Content marketing is like the running play in football. It's not flashy, people call it "old school," the fans don't like it, but it works!

PICK YOUR CONTENT FORMAT

Now, before we move on to how to actually plan out and create remarkable free content, I want you to think about what content format(s) will be a good fit for you. At their core, there are three types of content: written articles, videos, and audio podcasts. All three are fun and can be effective, and you certainly don't have to pick just one. But let me briefly point out the strengths and weaknesses of each.

	Pros	Cons
Podcasts	As an accepted long-form format, podcast listeners are highly engaged and tend to be very loyal.	Requires some basic knowledge of audio processing to ensure your podcast sounds professional.
	Can be more casual, needing little to no editing.	Requires a quiet space to record uninterrupted (i.e., you can't do it at the coffee shop).
	As it's audio only, there's no need to have a beautiful physical space or to get "camera ready."	No great way for your listeners to leave comments inside their favorite podcasting app, like Apple Podcast or Spotify.
	Only basic equipment needed—a decent USB podcasting microphone and some free software like Apple's Garageband or Audacity on Windows are all you need.	Not as discoverable as videos or blog posts. The current podcast landscape is a bunch of closed-loop environments that make getting in front of a new audience more difficult than with YouTube or a written article.

	Pros	Cons
Written Blog Posts	Great for search engine optimization (SEO) or showing up in Google.	Can take a long time if you aren't a fast writer.
	Easy to create anytime and anywhere; all you need is a laptop and an internet connection.	Not as engaging for the modern video-loving world.
	Virtually no equipment or start-up cost.	
	Very "skimmable" for people who want to quickly see if they like your content.	

	Pros	Cons
YouTube Videos	Very searchable in YouTube, great for discoverability.	Requires some equipment; a modern smartphone with a basic lavalier microphone can be totally professional if you have enough natural light.
	No website needed to get started; just create a free YouTube channel.	Requires basic video editing software and knowledge.
	Viewers can have a deeper connection with you as they can both hear and see your personality.	Requires a quiet and available physical space (again, can't do it at the local coffee shop).
	People have an insatiable appetite for video these days.	Requires having energy and a likeable personality (no offense if you don't have either).
		Requires getting dressed and doing your hair or makeup (not everyone is "camera ready" when they roll out of bed).

So now it's time to pick your format. I would encourage you to start with one format. You can always expand later if you so desire. **And if you are curious as to which one is *my* personal favorite, it's YouTube.**

While I have people who discover my blog posts and podcast regularly, I have personally seen faster growth on my YouTube channels than anywhere else. YouTube truly is a powerful search engine that has been huge for my discoverability. Pair that with the fact that being able to see and hear me on video creates a deep connection with my viewers and I'm set. I also love the built-in comments feature that gives me instant feedback on what my students like and want more of.

You can even combine formats simultaneously. If you go the podcast route, for example, I highly suggest either filming it and making it a video podcast (this is what I do) or creating a written blog post to go with it and hosting it on your own site.

Ultimately, what matters most is to start where you feel comfortable. It all works.

What's *more* important than content format is the content itself. What should your content be about? What if you run out of content ideas? Yeah, let's talk about that.

What Are Your Content Buckets?

Years ago when I started creating content for my first business, I felt like I had about twelve blog posts worth of ideas. That was it. I figured I could teach everything I know about recording and producing music in just twelve pieces of content. The idea that I could (and would) pump out content every week for the next twelve *years* would have seemed impossible back then.

If you are starting to feel overwhelmed as you project your business into the future simply because you're afraid you'll run out of content ideas, welcome to the club. Everyone feels this at one point or another. Fortunately, I have a solution for you: content buckets.

Instead of thinking about content as individual pieces, think of it in categories—or buckets. When you think about your topic or niche, what are four or five categories (or subtopics) that your people will want to learn about or need help with? Give yourself a few minutes to think about it now. I'm sure it will come quickly if you don't overthink it.

For example, if you were a fitness instructor creating an online business around that niche, your content buckets might look like this:

- workouts/exercises
- nutrition/eating
- recovery/sleep
- home gym equipment reviews

There's no right or wrong way to categorize or group your content into buckets. All that's important is that those buckets make sense to you and likely to your audience. The power of content buckets comes when you try and plan out some content ideas ahead of time. If you decide to post a new piece of content every week, for example, the planning process gets simpler. Instead of needing to come up with fifty-plus pieces of content every year, you simply need to come up with ten to twelve content ideas for each of your four to five buckets.

And honestly, that shouldn't be too hard. **Especially when you realize that the best content is simply answers to popular questions.**

Let's go back to the fitness instructor example. If she were sitting down to map out her content for the year, she would start with her first bucket: workouts/exercise. To quickly generate a list of content ideas, she could start by writing down every big question she ever gets about working out. They might look like this:

- Is cardio better than weight training?
- How long of a workout is necessary to get results?
- What is the best type of workout to burn fat?
- Will lifting weights make a woman look too bulky?

All of those questions would make great content topics. And they are all likely things her target audience is literally typing into Google right now. Our fitness instructor could likely fill up twelve or so content ideas for that category in a few minutes. Then all she would need to do is repeat that process for her remaining three buckets.

You can (and should) do the same for your niche. I highly suggest taking a couple of hours to sit down and think through the biggest questions your audience has for each of your content buckets and map out ten to twelve ideas for each of your four to five buckets. **The end goal is simple: around fifty content topics in a Google Doc somewhere.** Having these ideas bulleted out before you begin to launch your business gives you two powerful benefits:

1. **You don't have to think; you can just create.** When you get into the rhythm of posting new content, you won't be sitting in front of a blank screen, clueless as to what you should talk about next. Instead, you'll have a backlog of great ideas ready to pull from as you feel inspired.

2. **Your content will be more balanced as it rotates between each category or bucket.** I personally try and rotate through each bucket from post to post, as it ensures I hit all the key areas my audience wants help with. Granted, there's nothing wrong with doing some themed content over a period of time, but the bucket concept really gives you a well-rounded brand.

If you are still getting stuck with what content you should put in your buckets, go back to your research. What topics, questions, challenges, and dreams kept coming up in conversations with people on social, in book reviews, and in Facebook groups or forums?

Another great place to start is to simply copy (I mean, "get inspired by") what others in your niche are creating content on already. For example, look up a popular YouTube channel on your topic and sort their videos by most popular. Take note of what their top ten videos are about. Can you cover similar things? Can you do your own version of their videos? The answer is an obvious yes.

Once you get started jotting down content ideas in your buckets document, you'll get better at this. And once you begin actually *creating* content and interacting with your initial audience, the feedback you get in the comments and emails will prove to be an endless pool of new content ideas for the future. **Content creation online is a beautiful feedback loop. Pay attention and you will never run out of ideas.**

TWO SECRETS TO GREAT (AND EFFECTIVE) CONTENT

Now that you have your content buckets, I want to share two secrets I've learned to help you spice things up a bit so that your content actually gets noticed.

Secret #1: Be consistent.

The best content is consistently and predictably delivered. Like your favorite TV show, your audience can count on you to serve up something new regularly.

Search engines like Google and platforms like YouTube tend to favor websites and channels that consistently publish new, fresh content. And this makes sense given their job is to serve up relevant results when people search, and newer content will always be seen as more relevant than older content. Thus, a brand that is putting out new stuff regularly will get rewarded more than one that relies on content it made six years ago.

All you need to do is simply commit to a consistent rhythm of content output. This doesn't have to be every day, but it does need to be regular. It's no good to post a lot for a month and then disappear for three months. The brands that consistently publish week in and week out will win.

At minimum, I would shoot for one new piece of content a week. More is great if you can. But don't do less.

Secret #2: Be bold or polarizing.

The best content is opinionated, bold, or polarizing. Why? Because people remember it. Bold content connects emotionally with an audience. Safe content doesn't. If you really believe in something, then say it. If you really hate something, then say it. Don't talk around your beliefs; share them and teach them boldly.

Here are some simple questions to ask yourself to help generate bold content ideas:

- What methods or strategies in your niche are you for and against?
- Who are the "bad apples" in your industry?
- What is one idea in your field of experience you passionately believe that many people would disagree with you on?

Not all of your content needs to be polarizing, but you do need to mix this kind of stuff in so that your audience can either gain an even deeper attachment and affection for you or be repelled away. Repelling people who aren't a good fit for your brand is just as important as attracting those who are.

A great example of this is Dave Ramsey, the money coach and host of the nationally syndicated radio program *The Dave Ramsey Show*. Where most personal finance authors and radio hosts sound the same and are relatively boring, Dave says things like "Debt is dumb" and shuns the use of credit cards. Both of those stances would offend most Americans who have debt and credit cards. But this polarization works and has helped him build a multimillion-dollar empire.

THE 80/20 RULE OF CONTENT

You might be familiar with Pareto's principle, also known as the 80/20 rule. Simply put, this "rule" states that there are naturally occurring lopsided relationships in the world. Eighty percent of the world's wealth is owned by 20 percent of the world's population. Eighty percent of your revenue in business comes from 20 percent of your products or clients, and so on. The exact percentage is not what matters; instead, it's the fact that not everything is equal.

This applies to your content as well. **The truth is, even though you will publish great content each week for years and years, only a small handful of your videos or articles will send you the majority of your traffic and followers.**

And what's fascinating is you never know which pieces of content those will be. For example, a few years ago I published a video on whether you should form an LLC or stay a sole proprietor for your business. As of this writing, that single video accounts for over 20 percent of all my views. To me, that is such a random video because I don't dive deep into taxes and business structures on my channel. But for some reason, it ranks well with related search terms.

The lesson here? Commit to the process, knowing that you don't need to hit a home run every time. Most of your videos or blog posts will never go viral or bring in massive traffic. But you don't need them to. Even two or three big videos or blog posts can catapult your business to new heights and sustain you for years.

CONTENT MARKETING IS A LONG GAME

Now you know more than most people online about how to create truly remarkable content. And you might be excited to start writing or filming or podcasting. But I want to warn you of something. A content-marketing strategy takes time. You're playing the *long* game.

And most budding online business owners don't want to wait. They want instant results. They want an audience now, and they want income now. If I thought it was wise (and consistently successful) to take some shortcut to audience growth, I would be teaching you that, but it's not. Content marketing is the best method, in my opinion.

Remember: there are two huge benefits to being a content creator— you can build an audience of loyal fans who love everything you do, and you build credibility in the marketplace.

There is no shortcut to loyalty and credibility. But they are worth building toward.

When I started the Recording Revolution, no one knew who I was. I didn't have any A-list celebrities as my clients. I had no Grammy nominations or awards for albums I had produced. In reality, I was just a guy in my spare bedroom with an idea to try and help musicians make better-sounding recordings using budget equipment and simple strategies.

But now that I have hundreds of thousands of readers, viewers, and subscribers, I have a lot of credibility in the industry, which has opened many doors. Grammy-winning producers and musicians actually follow my stuff and want to connect with me. Why? Years of content creation has built that loyalty and credibility. It has turned me into a household name in my niche, and it can do the same for you. You might even get job offers as a result of your blog or channel. All because good content creates credibility for you.

Before we move on to the next chapter, we need to address something critical. Most content out there these days is garbage.

It's boring, obvious, and quite literally, unremarkable. This is because most people just don't try. They know that content is important, so they create it as quickly as they can without any thought of making something that will be fresh, timeless, and packed with value. But not you. You are going to stand out from the crowd by making really good, remarkable content. Here's how.

HOW TO CRAFT THE PERFECT BLOG (OR VIDEO) POST

When it comes to writing an effective and memorable blog post, it really comes down to two things: picking the right topic and crafting a compelling outline. Taking the time to put together a killer outline is well worth it.

It makes writing *much* faster, but more importantly, it ensures your post will be amazing. As you'll see, there are three key elements to crafting the perfect blog post, and this outline method will ensure you don't skip any.

When I sit down to write a post or outline a video, I begin with a simple, five-part template. I'll write a dummy title (likely to be tweaked later), and then below that, I map out these five sections:

- The Introduction
- Big Idea 1
- Big Idea 2
- Big Idea 3
- The Conclusion

Some posts might only have two points, and some have four, but 90 percent of the time, my posts follow this format: three main points sandwiched between an introduction and a conclusion. As simplistic as this might sound, each element to this outline has a purpose.

The Three Big Ideas

The meat of the post are the three points or the three big ideas. These are the things I want to teach or share in the post or video. Three points is a good number psychologically. **It flows easily like a story (beginning, middle, and end) and most people can remember and follow three ideas. Beyond that we begin to forget what we just learned.** So I like to keep my content to three main points or takeaways.

For example, if I were going to write a post about why I think a passive-income business is the best model for most people, I might have these three points:

1. It's low cost and easy to start.
2. It has high profit margins.
3. It provides ultimate flexibility.

In my outline, those would be the three middle elements where I would spend the bulk of my time teaching. They would be the three main things

I want people to remember. Now, within each of those three big ideas, I generally have three subpoints (see a pattern here?).

For example, in point 1 (passive-income businesses are low cost and easy to start), I would likely talk about what tools you actually need to start a business, then I would compare the cost to other business models, and finally, I would show how you can start one in your spare time while still keeping a day job. Three subpoints under the first main point. Make sense? In my outline, these would be three loose bullet points under each section.

The Introduction

Now let's go back to the first element of my outline: the introduction. This is so important as it's what sets up the rest of the post or video. We have to draw people in and give them a reason to keep reading (or watching).

A little tip here: generally speaking, there are three learning profiles out there: the *why* people, the *what* people, and the *how* people.

The *what* and the *how* people tend to jump right in, but if we don't start our post with *why* any of this matters, then a good chunk of your audience won't care to keep reading. We need to get to the heart of why this post or video will be worth their time. So I like to lead off with something intriguing and interesting that focuses on a benefit (or benefits) for the reader.

An example of an introduction for my passive-income post above might go like this:

> *"If you had told me ten years ago that I could be working five hours a week, have complete work freedom, and earn more than a doctor, I would have laughed in your face."*

It's a line that gets people's attention and sets us up to transition into the *what* and *how* of passive income. We might dive into the *why* a bit more and paint the picture of what having a passive-income business can feel like, but you get the idea. The introduction doesn't have to be long, but it does need to tee up the rest of the content so that people's mouths are watering and they're interested in what lies ahead.

The Conclusion

This is generally the easiest part of the outline, but how you do it is critical.

We want to briefly summarize any key points but then quickly transition over to the reader or viewer. What is the Action Step for them? What is the big lesson for them? What taste do you want to leave in their mouth?

This is your opportunity to leave a final thought that sticks with them and puts an exclamation point on your post. But that's not all; you need a CTA (call to action) to finish. What are you asking them to do now? Typically, there are two main CTAs that I end with for my content:

- opt-in for my lead magnet (more on lead magnets in the next chapter)
- a request to answer a specific question in a comment below

Both are great options because they further engagement and grow your email list. But the most important for you is the lead-magnet opt-in. So those are the five parts of the outline—but we're not done. There are two more elements to crafting a killer outline that leads to the perfect post, and they are value shots and the title.

Value Shots

Once you have your five-part outline in place, it's time to spice it up. We don't just want to deliver "good" content; we want to create the perfect post—something unique, memorable, and substantive. The best way to elevate any post is to add what are called value shots. This is a concept I learned from Ramit Sethi, and it's a game changer.

All we're doing here is looking at each of our three big ideas and seeing if we can add one element to each one to make it more interesting. Here are some examples of value shots:

- charts, graphs, or images
- relevant quote from someone

- a funny image or meme
- a personal story that's relevant
- an additional video that's relevant
- research or data on the subject
- humor in general

All I do is look at each big idea and ask myself: "*What value shot can I add here to drive this point home or make it more interesting?*" Sometimes, that's doing some more research and finding some data that really backs up my point. Other times, it's a funny cat meme. Many times, it's embedding or linking to a relevant video that I've done.

There are a million ways to do this, and it's so simple. But the effect is powerful because it adds value to each of your main points and creates a more substantive post or video.

In review, my outline will have three main points, each with an accompanying value shot. Now on to the final piece of the puzzle, which ironically is the first thing people will see: the title.

The Title

Once we have a better picture of where this post or video is going (because we've done our outline), it's time to put a bow on it with a compelling title. The title is critical because it's the first thing people see and it will determine whether they want to read or watch the post.

We have two goals here with the title: (1) clearly spell out what they can expect from this post and (2) create intrigue and curiosity.

The first goal is important: we want people to know what to expect. We don't want to be vague. If the post is all about passive income, we should probably mention that phrase or something that evokes the idea of online business and passive income. So don't get cute and try and trick your audience into clicking on your post. That's not a good long-term strategy.

At the same time, however, we don't have to be boring. We want to stand out when we can and draw people in with our titles. So it's a good idea to spice things up a bit with powerful words or create curiosity.

Here are three potential titles for my hypothetical passive-income post:

"How to Start a Passive-Income Business"
"The Truth About Passive Income"
"Passive Income: From Skeptic to Success Story"

Which of those titles is most appealing to you?

While the first one is totally fine, it's just average. I'm sure a million people have a post called exactly that. The second one is a bit more interesting because it seems to question the idea of passive income. The third, however, is my favorite, and for two reasons:

1. It likely appeals to skeptics and believers alike.
2. People love to hear about conversion/transformation stories.

If I went with the third title, I would likely need to make sure my introduction alluded to my perspective shift on passive income, and that might make it a bit longer, but other than that, my core content could stay the same.

Do you see what we did there? We crafted a headline that would appeal to more people while still being clear about the content inside.

There you have it: the three elements to crafting the perfect blog or video post.

- **Start with your five-part outline.**
- **Identify your three big ideas, each with its own subpoints. Then write an introduction that draws the reader in and a conclusion that points them to take action.**
- **Spice up your main points with value shots.**
- **Finally, craft a compelling title that is more likely to get clicks and shares.**

All of this work might sound like a lot. But it's worth it. Once you have your outline in place and fleshed out, writing the post is effortless. And the same is true for shooting a video. You know exactly what to say, and you know you've got a lot of value to offer. The result will be blog posts and videos that stand out from the crowd and hold their own for years to come. And, of course, this process applies perfectly to a podcast as well.

AUDIENCE BUILDING NEVER STOPS

In the next chapter, we'll dive into how to best build your website and, more importantly, grow your email list. But before we do, I have one final thing to point out regarding content. Audience building never stops. That means content creation never stops. Content is not merely a step on the path to creating an income stream that you cross off your list once you've been sharing some content for a year or two. **In fact, it's the *only* step in this six-step process that never ends.**

The great thing is that, as time goes by, you build more and more momentum online. This means that each new piece of content you create has even more potential impact, reach, and power to build your business.

My hope is that you take this to heart and commit to being a content creator from here on out as it will truly be what fuels the engine of your business for a long time (more on this in chapter 10).

Action Step:

Take some time to decide what content format you will start with. Then pick four to five content buckets or categories that you will create content around. Finally, make some notes outlining ten to twelve content ideas for each bucket.

Chapter 5

STEP 3: BUILD YOUR WEBSITE

Turn Online Visitors into Warm Leads

All this time, you might have been nervously wondering when we were going to talk about your website. Have no fear. In this chapter, I'm going to show you not only what tools to use for your site but also how to set up your website to be as effective as possible to grow your business.

But before I do, there's something controversial I must address.

What I'm about to share with you is one of the most important pieces of this online income puzzle, and yet it's the one most people dismiss as silly and unnecessary.

But those people would be dead wrong.

If you've been nodding your head and agreeing with me so far up to this point, this is the chapter where you might be tempted to laugh at me, close this book, and toss it on the shelf.

Here it is: email is more important than social media.

Most people think the opposite.

But again, they would be wrong. At least when it comes to running a business and making money. But how can I say that? Am I just out of touch? Email is so 1999, isn't it? Aren't we living in the age of social media now?

I get it. Trust me. We are light-years beyond the days of AOL telling you in robotic fashion, "You've got mail!" These days every business or brand wants a *huge* following on Facebook, Instagram, TikTok, and Twitter (and whatever new platform comes out next). But let me ask a not-so-obvious but all-important question:

Does having all those followers actually translate into making more money? Short answer: no.

Could it be that email (and by that, I mean specifically email marketing) is really where the money is made? Short answer: yes. Don't believe me? Let's pull the curtain back a bit and think critically about these two tools (social media and email) and why I believe email is where you should focus your efforts.

FOLLOWERS ARE BYSTANDERS—EMAIL SUBSCRIBERS ARE WARM LEADS

While social media seems to be the sexy tool to promote your business, email is still the dominant tool for actually putting money in your pocket, and I'll show you why. The truth about social media is that followers are bystanders. While email subscribers, on the other hand, are warm leads.

Think about it—it takes little commitment to click "Like" or "Follow" on social. A passing glance. A funny tweet or meme. Someone who clicks "Follow" is simply saying, "Yeah, I want to see a bit more of this." But that's all. They stand back and watch you from afar, with little commitment or buy-in to what your brand is all about.

Email subscribers, on the other hand, have taken things a whole step further—they have given you their email address. Their email address, people! **They are basically inviting you to contact them directly.** They are clearly interested in what you have to offer because, by subscribing, not only are they saying they like what you do, but also they want you to reach out to them with more.

This is what makes selling to your email list *far* more profitable than trying to sell and promote on social media.

According to a 2019 study from OptinMonster, email is the preferred channel for promotions by consumers (three times that of social media). It also has a three-times conversion rate of that of social media. And not only that, but also it has almost forty times the engagement rate that social media has.

The same article also went on to say this:

60 percent of consumers state that they have made a purchase as the result of a marketing message they received by email. On the flip side, only 12.5 percent of them even consider a buy button as a purchase driver on social media.

This is huge. Email drives sales far more than social media does. But it doesn't stop there. According to a December 2020 article on Emarketer.com, email leads social media as the most effective channel for customer retention by 20 percent.

Clearly, people love and use social media platforms. And, yes, they can be a great tool for connecting with your audience and staying top of mind (more on that in chapter 9). But the data continues to show that people are actually making purchases based on email promotions rather than social media posts. And this is because social media followers are bystanders, and email subscribers are warm leads.

The statistics alone should be enough to prove that email marketing is far more effective than social media marketing (paid or free), but there's more reason to focus on building an email list instead of a social media following.

SOCIAL MEDIA IS RENTING—EMAIL IS OWNING

Building a social media following is a lot like renting a house, while building an email list is like owning a house. Let me explain.

Social media platforms like Twitter, Facebook, and Instagram can (and do) change their rules and algorithms. They have control, not you. You can spend years building a substantial following on any of these platforms, and in the blink of an eye, you no longer have the ability to get in touch with those people. All because the rules were changed. Let me give you a personal example.

Just a few years ago, Facebook made a *huge* shift in their platform. At the time, if I posted something on my Recording Revolution Facebook page, all 100,000+ fans and followers would see that post at some point in their feed. Of course, they would have to log in to Facebook that day in order to see it, but my post was guaranteed to show up in their feed because they had chosen to follow or like my page.

Then one day things completely changed.

Facebook made a massive shift in their business model and subsequently altered their "rules" so that now only 13–18 percent of my followers or fans would see my posts "organically." If I wanted more people to see my content, I would have to "Boost" the post (i.e., pay Facebook) to show my content to my followers.

That's right, folks: I had to *pay* Facebook to connect with people who had already chosen to follow me.

The result? My web traffic to my site was cut in half in just twenty-four hours. That's a big deal when you run an online business. Traffic is your lifeblood. Fortunately for me, I don't rely exclusively on Facebook (or any social media platform) to earn income. And neither should you.

When you build your business on social media platforms, you are essentially building your business in someone else's world. You are playing in their sandbox. And they can change things in an instant. Or worse, those platforms can completely disappear or lose their popularity. Anyone remember MySpace? No? My point exactly. That site was *the* place to connect with fans.

Until it wasn't.

You and I have no idea what new platform will come and dethrone the current kings and queens of social media, thus rendering all of your hard work building a following useless. And with all the uncertainty of government involvement with these platforms lately regarding data and privacy, no social media app is permanent.

Email, on the other hand, is less like renting a house (where your land-lord can evict you or raise the rent) and more like home ownership (where you can do what you want in the house and your payment stays virtually the same). With email lists, you own the list. You can email your subscrib-ers anytime you like, without a middleman, no matter what social media platforms come and go (or how they change their algorithms).

You have the power to show up directly in your subscribers' inboxes, even if they never hop on social anymore. And the best part: most people rarely change their email addresses.

All the Big Brands Know This

You might be wondering if anyone else is aware that followers are like bystanders, and social media is like renting, while email subscribers are like warm leads, and your email list is like owning. You bet they are—*all* the big brands know this and are capitalizing on it.

Right now, go to just about any major brand's website where you like to shop and notice what happens. A pop-up will likely appear asking you to do something. And what are they asking you for? Is it to follow them on Instagram? Or to like them on Facebook? Nope. They want one thing and one thing only—your email address.

Oh, they'll give you something in exchange, of course. Twenty-five percent off your first order. Free shipping. An exclusive guide or video download. They will offer something you want in exchange for what *they* want —your email address.

And why are they doing this? Because they know what I just shared with you. **In order to sell more products and grow their businesses, they'd rather be in your inbox the moment they have a sale or new item available than hope you see them on social media.**

Even better, with email clients like Kajabi or Mailchimp, these big brands can track your habits, like which emails you open and which links you click on. All of that gives them the data they need to better sell to you.

So now that you know (and are hopefully starting to believe) that email marketing is more effective and therefore more important than social media promotion, it's time you start building your own email list. And it starts with building a website designed to do just that.

BUILD A WEBSITE THAT BUILDS YOUR LIST

Your business needs a website. Not a complicated website, not a perfect website. Just a good website. Specifically, one that is optimized for email-list building. What I want to do right now is give you the context for what your website needs (and doesn't need) in order to be effective for building your business. After that, I'll walk you through my favorite tools for actually building your site, quickly and easily.

Let's start with the harsh reality: most websites are one big, expensive business card. There's too much information about the owner/business and not enough about the customers and solving their problems.

The truth is, if you're lucky enough to have someone land on your website, you have only three seconds to grab their attention before they leave your site for good. In those three seconds, your visitor is trying to scan your site to quickly determine if you have something to offer them.

The solution? A powerful headline that states how you can help solve their problem. The headline is the most prominent text on the top of your website on what we call the "hero" image. You should be able to read the headline without having to scroll down on the site.

The headline is the most important text on your site because it's the only thing every site visitor is guaranteed to see. So what are the keys to an effective headline? Three things:

- **Be focused on the customer instead of on yourself and your brand.** Wanting to promote themselves first is one of the biggest mistakes people make. Doing so is completely backward. Your headline—and your entire website—should talk to *them* about *them*.

- **Clearly state the benefits (not features) of your solution.** Features are self-focused. Solutions are others-focused. People don't care about your products or service as much as they care about the solutions to their problems that you can offer.
- **Don't be vague.** Remember: you only have three seconds to grab their attention on your site, so you must be clear. Author and marketer Donald Miller always says, "When you confuse, you lose." Clarity matters here. For example, I once saw this headline on a website: "Discovering your greatness one day at a time." What does that even mean?

So what are some examples of a good headline? Here are three very different, but equally effective, headlines to learn from.

"How to generate 195,013 visitors a month without spending a dollar on ads."

This is from Neil Patel, who is an online marketer who specializes in content and SEO. If you land on his site and are trying to get more people to your *own* website, then that headline is quite appealing. It's also very clear what he is all about and how he can help your business.

"Superfast and Secure Wordpress Hosting + Content Marketing and SEO Tools?"

This is a headline from a web-hosting company called Web Synthesis. In one sentence (posed as a question), they have told you that they can solve your problem of slow and unsecure hosting for your WordPress site. They even can help you with content marketing and search engine optimization. Again, it's super clear who this site is for.

"Create Radio-Worthy Songs from Your Bedroom or Home Studio."

This is one of my own for Recording Revolution, my brand dedicated to helping musicians make great sounding recordings at home with budget equipment. The promise is clear: I can help you make songs that sound like they belong on the radio, all from your lowly bedroom recording studio.

Do you see how having done all that research and committing to creating regular content week in and week out will give you a deep enough understanding of who you are helping and what you can help them do? All of that allows you to craft a powerful and effective headline that draws a visitor deeper into your site and gives you a chance to do what your site is truly built to do.

THE POWER OF LEAD MAGNETS

Most websites give visitors too many options, which only distract them. Instead of telling them to follow you on Facebook or Instagram, or read your About page, your website should focus on one thing—capturing visitors' email addresses.

If they leave without giving you their email address, they will likely never come back. It's just true. **Remember: if you were lucky enough that they found you in the ever-growing sea of digital content, then you can't bank on being lucky enough that they will find their way back in the future.** People rarely bookmark websites anymore; they simply move on. But we can't let that happen.

If you capture their email address before they disappear for good, you now have an open door. You can email them exclusive content or point them to your latest post or video to add more value for free, thereby creating a relationship. Eventually, you can offer them your products or services and sell directly through email or point them back to the site.

So the question you might be asking is: How do I collect their email address?

First, I can tell you what *not* to do. Don't simply put up an email opt-in form and say, "Join our newsletter!" Nobody wants to join an email list. Nobody wants to read another email newsletter. In fact, nobody really wants more email in their inbox. So why in the world would someone offer you their email address so willingly? Because you're going to give them something in exchange for it.

If someone lands on our website, we want to immediately offer them a gift. Specifically, a benefit-driven lead magnet. And what is a lead magnet, you might ask? **Quite simply, a lead magnet is something that will immediately help someone solve a problem.**

This is the beginning of the value circle we talked about in chapter 2. Your goal is to show them you have massive value to offer and give it for free in exchange for their email address. It's easy to do, and best of all, it works.

And here's the thing: a lead magnet is just another piece of content. It's just like your YouTube videos, podcast episodes, or blog posts. The only difference is it's not available to the public without them opting into your email list.

Let me give you some examples of lead magnets you can create that have proven to be very effective for me and my students over the years. If you are getting stuck coming up with ideas for your first lead magnet (your free offering that you give away in exchange for an email address), these might help.

Five Irresistible Lead-Magnet Ideas

I've built all kinds of lead magnets over the years: videos, e-books, PDF guides, and podcast-style audio trainings. And to be honest, the format doesn't matter nearly as much as the content inside.

What makes a lead magnet irresistible is the promise it delivers—the solution it offers.

The promise you choose to make will come primarily from doing your research and finding out what people need help with and what their desires are. Here are five simple templates you can use as a jumping-off point to get your first lead magnet going.

The Multistep Guide

Example: *"Six Steps to a Radio-Ready Song Guide"*

This is a classic lead-magnet idea. Simply focus on giving your audience five steps (or three or four or seven, etc.) that they can follow to achieve a desired result.

What is a solution they are looking for in your niche that you can map out in a simple PDF guide (three to ten pages, tops) giving them the necessary steps to get there? The number of steps doesn't matter. Just that it is a concrete number and will lead to a benefit or solution they want. And be specific on what the benefit is.

The Cheat Sheet or Checklist

Example: *"Graham's Compression Checklist: Seven Strategies for Using Compression"*

Even easier than the multistep guide is the cheat sheet or checklist. This is a simple one- to two-page PDF that literally lists out quick and easy strategies, rules, tips, techniques, or hacks that your audience can use right away.

These do not have to be in-depth, but simply packed with helpful and easy-to-implement ideas on your topic. In fact, they convert so well because people *know* that they aren't too in-depth—just quick wins.

The Stacked Benefit How-To

Example: *"How to Earn $1,000/Month of Passive Income in Just Thirty Minutes a Day"*

This lead magnet is a little more straightforward. Here you aren't focusing on specific steps per se, but rather giving them a clear how-to guide. The power, though, is in stacking a second benefit to the core benefit. So you are showing them how to get one benefit while also adding another: how to benefit + benefit.

My lead magnet "How to Earn $1,000/Month of Passive Income [one benefit] in Just Thirty Minutes a Day [another benefit]" is a good example of this. Another would be something like "How to lose five pounds a week without any exercise." It starts with "How to lose five pounds a week" (one benefit) "without any exercise" (another benefit).

The Ultimate Guide

Example: *"The Ultimate Guide to Email Copywriting"*

This is the complete opposite of the cheat sheet or checklist lead magnet. Instead of short, quick, and easy to digest, the ultimate guide is long, in-depth, and "complete." That's the appeal, that it is the "ultimate guide" to whatever your topic is.

It feels authoritative and helpful because the reader will have everything she needs in one easy-to-reference PDF. I'll be honest: these aren't my favorite for a *first* lead magnet because they take so long to create, but they can be effective to add to your arsenal later.

"The Multiday Challenge"
Example: *"The Seven-Day Mind, Body, Heart Challenge"*
This is a powerful lead magnet for many people because it isn't just information, but motivation and accountability. Instead of giving them a PDF guide, you are sending them a series of emails over the course of the number of days in the challenge.

Each day, they receive a new step, with a new action for that day's challenge. It draws the reader in and moves them along this journey to a desired result. One thing that is unique about this type of lead magnet is that it also can act as your autoresponder (more on this in chapter 8), doing the work of teaching and priming the reader before you announce your product (assuming you've built one).

THE TOOLS YOU NEED TO BUILD YOUR WEBSITE AND EMAIL LIST

Now that I've made the case that you need an email list of warm leads to promote your future products and that your website should be created in such a way that it gets people to join your list, let's get technical and actually build your site and list.

I'll start with what tools I recommend for the job, and then I'll give you some helpful suggestions on how to build a beautiful, professional, and functional website. Quick caveat here: there are *many* great tools to choose from. This is not an exhaustive list. It contains my personal favorites (because of cost, simplicity, or both).

Website Builder

- **WordPress.** This is a free platform that has endless free and paid themes to start with. It is widely used and supported worldwide, which means there are tons of tutorials, support forums, and cool integrations that exist online.

If you go in this direction, you will need to pay for monthly web hosting through a company like GoDaddy to secure your space on the internet for your website to live. Basic hosting can be had for as cheap as six dollars a month. You will also need to buy your domain name (i.e., MyAwesomeBusiness.com), which is usually a twelve-dollar yearly fee.

The pros of WordPress are its low cost, vast customization ability, and well-thought-out blogging platform. But its cons are that it's a bit clunky, and your experience with the website builder really depends on the theme you go with. If you go the WordPress route, I highly recommend investing ninety-nine dollars or so on a premium theme, like Beaver Builder or Divi.

- **Squarespace.** If you prefer something with an easier-to-use visual editor, then this platform might be for you. For only twelve dollars/month, you get web hosting, a domain name, and a very pretty website builder.

  It's a bit more limited than WordPress in that you can't add a bunch of third-party plugins to customize your site's look and feature set, but everything is easier to use since it's all integrated into your Squarespace log-in. Plus, the site themes and designs truly are beautiful and professional.

- **Kajabi.** If you are willing to spend a bit more from the start, you can have what I believe to be the ultimate tool for your entire online business. Kajabi is a website builder with powerful themes and customization, but it's also your web hosting, email-list provider, digital-course builder, webinar platform, and customer portal.

  Starting at $119/month if you go with their annual plan, **Kajabi is certainly pricer than WordPress or Squarespace, but it eliminates the need for any of the other tools you will have to pay for.** I personally have moved both of my businesses from WordPress to Kajabi, and not only am I saving money, but also my life is easier, and I'm having more fun.

I'm going to be recommending Kajabi more as we go, but in case you want to try it out for yourself for free, I'd like to offer you a thirty-day free trial with my personal affiliate link. Just for using my link, I will also immediately send you my exclusive mini course "Ready Set Kajabi" absolutely free as a gift. And if you decide to become a paying Kajabi customer after your free trial, part of your payment comes back to support me, at no charge to you.

Just head over to www.GrahamCochrane.com/kajabi to grab your free trial and bonus course.

Now that your website is covered, you'll need to sign up for an email-list provider or email marketing service to begin collecting email addresses, setting up powerful email funnels (more on these in chapter 8), and sending out weekly broadcasts to your list. Here are three options I recommend.

Email Marketing Service

- **Mailchimp.** This is the email marketing platform I started with years ago. The great thing about Mailchimp is that you can get started for free and build a list of up to two thousand people. If you want more features (and more people on your list), then you will have to move to one of their paid plans, but it's a great option if you are starting out.

  People say that Mailchimp is too basic, and that might be true when compared to some of its competitors, but I used it for a long time and was making multiple six figures a year on the platform. Don't let basic hold you back from making money.

- **ConvertKit.** After seven years on Mailchimp, I eventually moved my list over to ConvertKit. This is a great platform with powerful automation and segmentation tools that ultimately won me over. As your business grows, having more precise control over who gets which emails becomes very desirable as it allows you to offer your subscribers a more tailored brand experience. Plus, it helps you make more money.

ConvertKit has a free plan as well (up to one thousand subscribers), but like Mailchimp, to access all their powerful automation tools, you'll have to move to their paid plans. As your list grows, so does your payment. But if you build your business right, your income should grow along with your list growth.

- **Kajabi.** And here we are again with Kajabi. The all-in-one platform that I use for my website, I also now use for my email marketing. And for two reasons: one, it works great and integrates with my online courses (which are built with Kajabi), and two, it's free.

  That's right: email marketing that is just as powerful as ConvertKit and the others is baked into your price as a Kajabi user. That is a huge savings when your list gets to be in the tens of thousands. At one point, I was spending over $2,000 a month on an email list of over three hundred thousand people. I moved that list to Kajabi and now spend zero dollars a month to market to the same list.

  Again, you can get thirty days free on Kajabi and a bonus mini course with my link. Just head over to www.GrahamCochrane.com/kajabi to get started for free.

Now that you know what tools you need to build your website and begin collecting email addresses, let me give you the quick rundown on everything your website should include. Ironically, it's not much.

THE FIVE ELEMENTS YOUR WEBSITE NEEDS

1. **Home page that offers your lead magnet.** When people type in YourAwesomeBusiness.com, they will land on your home page. This is your first impression and the most important page on

your site. The goal here is simple: grab their attention and offer your lead magnet.

Common things to include on this page are a benefit-driven headline, a subheadline that gives more detail on the lead-magnet promise, an opt-in box or form for visitors' email addresses, a nice headshot of you, and perhaps more specifics on what solution your lead magnet offers them. The goal of this page is to communicate who you help and what you help them do, and ultimately capture an email address. Nothing more, nothing less.

2. **About page.** If people like what they see on the home page but want to know more about who you are and what you offer, they might click on your about page. But let me tell you a secret that few ever realize: the about page is not meant to be about you. It should be all about your visitor.

    What this means is a good about page should instantly connect with your prospect and identify their pains, problems, hopes, or dreams. The goal of this page is to make them feel heard, understood, and appreciated. It should help your visitor know that she is in the right (or wrong) place. In essence, tell them what your site and your business is all about—which is helping them.

3. **Blog/content page.** Whether you choose to write articles, produce YouTube videos, or host a podcast, your site should have a blog page that publishes all your weekly content. I personally don't write blog posts anymore. However, I do publish a new post each week that embeds my latest YouTube video in it. You can do the same if you have a podcast.

    A blog/content page is important for two reasons. First, if someone discovers you through your website, you want them to be able to see your latest content without having to leave your site. So embed your latest video or podcast episode in a post and put it on display. Second, having your content live on your site will help you show up in Google search results, which helps you get discovered and grow your audience.

4. **Contact page.** Likely the easiest page to create, your contact page is where you give people a way to reach out to you directly via email. You can do this by listing your email address on the page or including a simple contact form. Either works great.

5. **Pop-up.** Finally, you'll want to add a pop-up or light box to your site. This is simply a box that appears within a few seconds of people landing on your site or when they try to leave your site that offers them your lead magnet. Whether you're using WordPress, Squarespace, or Kajabi, you can create a simple email opt-in pop-up and connect it to your email marketing tool of choice. Again, Kajabi makes this super easy because it is both your website builder and your email marketing provider.

Also, **I highly recommend that you insert an email opt-in form that promotes your lead magnet on every page on your site**. On the about page, the contact page, and after every blog post, you should mention your lead magnet. This can all be set up at once when building your site, and it truly helps you maximize every moment a visitor spends on your site.

When it comes to capturing email addresses these days, it's critical that you make clear to your visitor that by opting in they are agreeing to sign up for your list and get your weekly content emails. Simply having a line of text below the opt-in box that reads something to the effect of "*When you sign up, we'll be sending you weekly emails with additional free content*" will suffice.

What About Visual Style? Does It Matter?

When it comes to how your website should actually *look*, there's good news. All of today's website builders already come with beautiful, professional-looking designs that do all of the hard work for you. All you have to do is click, drag, and tweak to your liking. But I do have just two simple rules of thumb that will help ensure your site looks its best no matter what design you start with.

- **For credibility, it's best to use no more than two primary colors for your website's text and buttons:** one main color and one for links or buttons. You might be able to get away with three colors, but really any more than two and you are bound to make a mess of things.
- **The same goes for fonts: only use two.** Choose one for your headlines and the other for your main body text. A classic hallmark of amateur design is multiple mismatched fonts. Even if you can't tell yourself, trust me on this.

Again, if you start with the professionally designed themes in Kajabi, Squarespace, or WordPress, you'll be in good shape. Just don't mess up what they have going for them and keep it simple.

PROMOTE YOUR LEAD MAGNET EVERYWHERE

One final but important thought here is this: your lead magnet is the most important thing you could promote publicly. Whether on social media, at the end of your YouTube video or latest podcast episode, or even if you're being interviewed on someone else's platform, **when given the option to call people to action, the action you want them to take is to download your lead magnet**.

Remember: email-list building is critical to making money. So as you create more content and grow your audience, always call that audience to go deeper in the relationship with you by downloading your guide, cheat sheet, video workshop, and so on.

One pro tip to make this easier is to purchase an easy-to-remember and easy-to-spell domain name that can forward to a lead magnet opt-in page on your website. For example, I bought and use RadioReadyGuide.com, which simply points people to a Kajabi landing page that offers my lead magnet. On the other hand, you can simply use a short page name like GrahamCochrane.com/workshop to do the same thing.

Either way, the point is to promote your lead magnet in your content and everywhere else you teach or add value as the next logical step for them if they liked what they received from you so far. And the great thing is, it's an easy offer because it's a gift. I love giving away free stuff, don't you?

And if you're concerned about what you should be emailing to your list, don't worry. For now, just begin the process of building your email list as you build your audience online. We'll go into detail in a bit on how you should interact with your email subscribers.

LET'S BUILD YOUR FIRST PRODUCT

Now that you're armed with the knowledge of how to build a website and begin growing your email list, it's time to (finally) create something to sell to your loyal audience. In the next chapter, I'm going to walk you through the process of creating your first online course or membership product using the amazing cheap and free tools we have at our disposal today.

But what is *inside* your digital product is critical. The worst thing that could happen is that you spend time, energy, and money building a product only to have no one buy it. We don't want that. The key is to only build a product that is virtually guaranteed to sell, which is not nearly as hard as it sounds.

For now, here is your Action Step. Actually, this time it's two:

Come up with your first lead-magnet idea by answering the question "What is one simple, burning pain I could solve for my audience that would give them an instant win?" Start outlining what you would cover in that lead magnet.

Second, decide which website builder and email marketing platform you will use for your online business. Create your account and start playing around with the tools inside.

Chapter 6

STEP 4: CRAFT YOUR PRODUCT

How to Create Your First Online Course or Membership

Over the past few years, I've noticed a trend in business-coaching advice, whether in books, videos, or courses. There is an overemphasis on the product side and an underemphasis on the "who to sell it to" side.

The typical business guru draws you in with all this talk about how much money you can make selling courses, or drop shipping on Amazon, but then somehow fails to mention that the greatest product in the world will make you zero dollars if you have no one to sell it to.

And this, my friend, is why we've worked so hard to build your audience and your email list *long* before we even spoke about what we would sell. Remember that without an audience nothing is possible, but with an audience, anything is possible. Now is the time, with your audience in hand, to make some money.

THE SIX MONETIZATION MODELS

Once you are getting regular traffic to your website and email subscribers on your list, it's time to monetize. But *how* you do so matters. There are six key ways to monetize your audience.

1. **Advertising/Sponsorships.** One of the easiest ways to make money is to run banner ads on your site or sponsorships on your YouTube videos or podcast. With people reading your website, watching your videos, or listening to your podcast all the time, you have something valuable to *other* businesses: eyeballs (or ears)!

   The key here is to find products and services that would be a natural fit for your audience and then pitch those companies to pay you monthly (or per post) to mention their brand and product. This monetization model has been around for decades, beginning in newspapers, radio, and TV commercials.

2. **Affiliate Marketing.** Another easy way to make money without a product of your own is to promote someone else's product as an affiliate. This is different from advertising in that you aren't paid to promote it, but rather you are paid a cut when someone buys it through your special affiliate link.

   A lot of online content creators do this by recommending tools or products they use. For example, photography educators might recommend a certain lighting kit on Amazon and then include their Amazon affiliate link in their YouTube description so if a viewer clicks through and buys the kit, the content creator earns a percentage of the sale.

3. **Crowdfunding.** A really cool way to monetize your content these days is through a crowdfunding platform like Patreon. With this model, you ask your superfans to support you financially on an ongoing monthly basis. Fans love to support their favorite content creators directly and usually receive some exclusive content or access in return.

One of my friends is a singer and performer who makes amazing a cappella covers of popular songs on YouTube. He films elaborate music videos and posts them for free every two weeks, but makes a full-time living on Patreon from his fans.

4. **Freelance Service.** Something amazing happens when you create content for a hungry audience—they begin to trust you, and you build amazing credibility. This can create a steady stream of warm leads for your service-based business. In fact, that's the first monetization model I ever had.

   I originally began blogging and creating videos on music recording years ago with the express purpose of landing new audio clients. It worked. My name got out there, and I was able to land clients all over the world who never would have heard of me otherwise.

5. **Consulting/Coaching.** Very similar to the freelance model is the consulting model. But rather than offering a service, you instead offer your expertise and experience to your clients. Again, your content gives you credibility and helps you become discovered by your ideal client.

   I've done consulting as well as business coaching. My content helps clients discover me. They join my email list or reach out to me from the website. Then these clients pay me for my time and advice. I don't do the work in their business for them, but rather, I coach them through the process.

6. **Products.** And finally we have the product model. This is pretty straightforward. You build your own original products and sell them to customers.

Just reading through those monetization models should be both eye-opening and exciting. As you build your audience, you can see all the income-earning potential at your disposal. The power of audience building is real, and the more you establish yourself online, the more opportunities will come your way. But I want to focus on one model that I think will serve you the most.

While all six models work and have their advantages—and I have used all of them myself—the holy grail of monetization (and my personal favorite) is products. This is because, with products, you no longer trade your time for money. There's a limit to how many clients you can take and how much you can charge, but there's no limit to how much product you can sell.

PRINTING MONEY OUT OF THIN AIR WITH DIGITAL PRODUCTS

But as much as I love products, personally I'm not a fan of *physical* products. They require lots of up-front money, storage, packaging, and shipping costs. *Digital* products are a different animal entirely. They cost little to create and maintain and can be sold to anyone, anywhere, at any time, and in unlimited quantities. When you create and sell a digital product, it's like printing money out of thin air.

Here are some examples of digital products you could create:

- online video courses
- e-books
- digital prints
- smartphone apps
- web tools
- membership sites

While all of these digital products can be great for your business, I can tell you that online video courses are my favorite type of digital product. Put simply, if you had to focus on only *one* type of digital product (especially when starting), this would be it.

YOUR FIRST PRODUCT SHOULD BE AN ONLINE VIDEO COURSE

There's a lot of talk these days about online courses and why they are so great. And for good reason: they *are* great. More specifically, I think they are great for the new online business owner and will serve you well. Here are five reasons why:

- **They are easy to build.** Since it's video, you can create the content much faster and more easily on your smartphone or with slides on your computer than writing a book or designing software.
- **They are easy to update.** Want to add more modules or update your course with new content? Just add to it in a snap and all your current customers get the new stuff.
- **You can teach better with video.** While books and e-books are a great way to share and teach information, video is even more effective than written content, because by adding the visual and auditory element of you being on camera or presenting slides, you keep your students more engaged by layering in two more senses to the experience. This leads to better customer results.
- **They allow for interaction.** Building an online course with something like Kajabi allows for students to ask questions, leave comments, and get feedback from you, the instructor.
- **You can charge more.** Compared to a book or an app, there is a much higher perceived value when offering an online video course. It compares more to a university class—but is even better than a class because it's self-paced.

But here is the best reason of them all: once they are built, online video courses are completely hands off and automatic. As I'll teach you in chapter 8, you can set your course up in an automated email funnel and have it selling for you worldwide, 24/7, even when you are sleeping or on vacation.

What about membership sites? A close second to online courses would be continuity programs or membership sites. While these are powerful products to offer (and I run a few myself), I don't recommend these until after you have at least one fully automated online course. At the end of this chapter, I'll outline some key things to consider when you feel ready to launch a membership site, but for now, I want you to focus on an online video course.

Now, when I say video course, what comes to mind?

Does the idea of filming an online course seem overwhelming, complicated, or stressful to you? Perhaps you've taken some courses yourself, and the production quality seemed so high or the sheer amount of content seemed daunting to create on your own. Have no fear. There are a few common misconceptions when it comes to creating online courses that I'd like to clear up for you now.

Misconception #1—You need a professional film crew.

While you certainly *can* hire a videographer to film your course, you don't need to. It certainly won't have any effect on whether your course sells or not. I've never hired anyone to build my courses. All you need is your smartphone and free software on your computer. That's it. (More on this in a moment.)

Misconception #2—They need to be really long and in-depth.

This comes from an insecurity that the value of a course is in how long it is. This couldn't be further from the truth. What makes a course valuable is the content and whether it helps students get results. Your course doesn't need to fit some certain length of time, but rather should be focused on providing valuable, in-depth information. Some of the best courses include two hours or less of video content. That's just eight videos of fifteen minutes in length.

Misconception #3—You need fancy online tools.

The good news is that you are living in the greatest time to be an online course creator. These days, very minor technical skill or knowledge is required. All you need is a platform like Kajabi. Or you can do it yourself with a free WordPress site, video embedding through a platform like Wistia or Vimeo, and a password-protection plugin. Even if you don't know these tools now, you can easily learn them.

With those misconceptions out of the way, here is my goal for you at this point: **build your first online video course as the logical next step after your free content and lead magnet for your students**. The flow of your online business and customer journey should look like this:

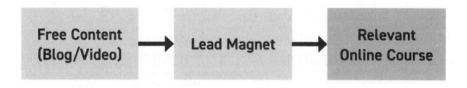

IT'S TIME FOR SOME MORE RESEARCH

So now that I've (hopefully) convinced you to build an online course, I want to say something pretty frank: **most online courses will fail to sell**.

Depressing? Maybe. But there's a lesson here that I want you to learn because I believe you have something valuable to share with the world and I want you to become wildly successful doing that.

The number one reason most products don't sell is because business owners build their products in a vacuum without doing any research. Remember: if you build it, they will (not) come. Never build a product and assume the "right" people will come begging for it. You'll waste both time and money.

The only way to virtually guarantee your product will sell is to do some strategic customer research and determine what people want to buy, and then go and build that for them.

By now, research hopefully won't feel like a dirty word to you. You've done it early on in your online business journey to discover what niche to build your brand around, and you're doing it informally as you learn what kind of content your audience wants to see. Now we're going to do a bit more to ensure that we build a product your people truly want to buy utilizing two simple methods.

Method #1—Informal Research

When it comes to researching for your first online course, there's no need to make things complicated. Simply paying attention to what your audience is already saying can go a long way toward building the right course on the right topic. Here are some suggestions of places to look and what to pay attention to.

- **Most popular content.** Which of your videos gets the most views? Which articles get the most comments? Where do you see the most engagement? These are clues as to what topic(s) your audience likely would pay for more in-depth training on.
- **Most common questions.** What questions do you hear from students/customers the most via email, comments, or social media? Is there a pattern or trend? Questions demand answers, and your online course could be the answer to their most burning question.
- **What your audience is already buying.** Sometimes, a competitor is offering a product that's missing from your offerings and your customers/audience are spending money with them. This is a big clue. If there is a type of course your audience is already buying from someone else, there's a good chance they would want to buy your version of the same thing because they like learning from you.
- **Frustrations.** Anytime you see language being used that communicates passionate frustration, pay attention. There is a problem waiting to be solved and your product could offer that solution.
- **Wants and wishes.** If you see someone saying, "I just wish I could . . ." or "I really just want to be able to . . . ," pay attention. They're asking for a product that helps them realize those desires.
- **Deeper motivations.** Get on social media or email and go back and forth as deep as you can with a few of your students. Ask them what they want or need. Then ask why over and over till you get to the core of what they truly want or need.

Method #2—Formal Surveys

Once you've done your first round of research, you should have a good idea of a few topics your first course could be built around. Now it's time to further clarify things by asking more direct questions using a formal survey.

- **Survey your email list.** Create a brief survey with Google Forms (which is a free tool) and email it out to your list. This survey should have questions geared to their current frustrations, desires, and so on.
- **Keep it short.** The fewer questions, the better, as people are busy and will get irritated if the survey is too long. Give them mostly multiple-choice questions because they're the fastest to answer.
- **Incentivize them to fill it out.** I usually offer to give away something awesome with a random drawing to entice people to fill out the survey. This could be a one-hundred-dollar gift card to a relevant store or website or a free sixty-minute coaching call with you. A little incentive can go a long way to getting participation.
- **Use multiple-choice questions (to get percentages).** These should be leading questions about what type of products they currently have and like, what they feel they need or want the most right now, and what their biggest problem is at the moment. With a tool like Google Forms, you can get pie charts that automatically update with each survey submission, showing you instantly and visually what your people want the most.
- **Include an open-ended question (to get their actual words).** Having at least one final question where respondents can write out their answer in their own words will give you powerful material to use when creating sales copy (more on that in chapter 9).

After going through all the research and surveys, try to narrow it down to three of the most desirable products based on what people have said. Either go with the top requested idea or one of those top three that interests you the most. The great news is that you now know that you are building a course around something your audience really cares about. On top of that, you will have a ton of helpful data to help you decide what specifically should go in the course as well.

THE SECRET TO A GREAT ONLINE COURSE

By doing the research, you are already miles ahead of most online course creators because you know you're building a course people want to buy. But it's still not time to begin filming. There is one more crucial step to creating an amazing course: creating a great outline.

Before you even begin to build, shoot, or create a single module of a course or product, you must create an outline that is enticing and irresistible to your target audience.

What do I mean by that? **If simply reading the outline of your course could make someone want to buy, then you're on the right track.**

So how do you create a mouthwatering course outline? There are two strategies I employ that do the trick every time.

The Bookstore Strategy

Imagine you walk into your favorite bookstore looking for a book on marriage. You're either newly engaged, newly married, or looking for more spark in your marriage. Whatever the case, you need help, and you're on a mission to find a good marriage book.

Naturally, you would navigate to the relationship section of the bookstore and begin searching. And what would you look at first? Book titles! That's the first thing you see. Even before you see the cover of many books, you see the title on the spine. Therefore, the title has to grab you in order for you to pull it off the shelf.

If you saw two marriage books side by side and one was titled "Marriage 101" and the other was titled "Three Simple Steps to an Effortlessly Joy-Filled Marriage," which one would you pick up? Uh-huh.

To begin your course outline, you need to come up with a compelling "must-have" title. With all the other "books" on the shelf, yours needs to have a more compelling title to even make someone want to pick it up.

If you happen to pick up the marriage book, what are you going to look at next before determining whether you should buy it? The table of contents. You want to know what the book will cover, and the chapter titles will tell you a lot about what to expect.

And if the chapters are titled something like "Marriage Basics" or "Stop Being Selfish in Your Marriage," you might put the book back on the shelf and move on. But if the chapters were titled something more like "How to Defuse Any Argument in Thirty Seconds" or "The Secret to Staying Sexy in the Eyes of Your Spouse," you might keep reading or go straight to the checkout counter and buy a copy.

So the analogy continues. If the first step to a great product outline is a great title, then the next step is to create a "must-have" table of contents. **Your job is to create names for each "chapter" or video module that are both descriptive and appealing to your ideal customer.** And when you think you have good titles, make them better. Revise the product and module titles over and over until they are literally irresistible to a potential customer.

How to Write Irresistible Video-Module Titles

If you've never written titles before and need some help coming up with something truly catchy, then consider the power of two-part titles. Start with a two- or three-word catchy title, followed by a colon, and then a longer, more descriptive phrase. Tim Ferriss, author of *The 4-Hour Work Week,* is a master at this. Here are some examples from that book:

- "Disappearing Act: How to Escape the Office"
- "Muse Math: Predicting the Revenue of Any Product"
- "The Holy Grail: How to Outsource the Inbox and Never Check Email Again"

Or just keep it simple and solution focused. Describe the benefit of that video or module but spice it up with some hyperbole, alliteration, or descriptive words. Here are some from one of my courses for my Recording Revolution brand:

- "The Building Blocks of a Bulletproof Home Studio"
- "The Ten Commandments of Killer Guitar Tone"
- "Get That Diva-Worthy Vocal Without All the Drama"
- "Leverage the Magic of Virtual Consoles and Tape"

Your first round of title ideas might not be the best, but it's better to get them down on paper and tweak them later than to wait until you have the *perfect* title. Write what you think is appealing, and then edit it to make it better.

The One-Hundred-Benefits Strategy

The second strategy I like to use when coming up with online course outlines is something I learned from speaker and author Brendon Burchard called the list of one hundred benefits. This is an exercise that I have found both difficult and exciting, but when utilized, the result is a much more desirable product for your customers.

The premise is simple: think about your online course in terms of benefits to your customer. Instead of focusing on what your course will teach, focus on what benefits your students will receive from working through the material.

Specifically, Brendon suggests you list one hundred benefits your customers will get from your course. If this sounds impossible, it is.

The first time I tried this exercise, I think I got to around seventeen benefits after thirty minutes of really trying. And that's the point. You can do more. You *should* do more to make your course as powerful as it can be. **If you run out of ideas (like I did), then create more benefits and then build them into the product.**

You can see why this is so powerful. It forces you to be benefit driven. With product creation, we typically become feature driven. But features don't sell; benefits and solutions do. This exercise keeps you focused on the latter.

It also reveals if your product isn't good enough. If you can't think of more than ten benefits, then your product isn't good enough to build yet. That's good to know now rather than later when you're trying to sell it to your email list.

This exercise inherently forces you to come up with new ideas. When you're trying to "come up with benefits," you think of really cool ideas for relevant topics that you may have missed or bonuses you could include with the course.

And what I think is most profoundly helpful about the exercise is that it gives you a list of benefits you can use in your marketing and sales copy later. This is the stuff that will actually get people to pull out their wallets and give you their money. By listing these benefits (and creating more of them), you, in essence, are drafting the foundations of a great sales page or email. You're doing the work of selling ahead of time.

In the end, great products come from a simple two-part process:

1. Deep customer research
2. Benefit-driven outlines

Once you've done the research and drafted up a highly desirable course outline based around all the benefits your customer will get from the course, it's time to actually film the darn thing.

How to Film Your Product for Cheap (or Free)

Filming video courses is where many people get hung up. They don't consider themselves videographers, and so they think that their options are to either hire a professional (costing thousands of dollars) or to do it themselves and have an amateur-looking and -sounding result. It turns out there's a third option: film it yourself for next to nothing (or entirely free) and with amazing results.

Trust me on this: you can DIY your videos and have them turn out great. But first, you have to decide what type of videos you need for your course. There are two distinct video styles for an online course, and each has strengths and weaknesses.

Video Style #1—Talking Head

This type of video is what many imagine when it comes to filming an online course. With talking head–style shots, you're facing the camera, usually framed from the chest up, and talking directly to the audience. Talking head videos are great for online courses (or just specific video modules) that only require communicating content without any supporting images, data, or examples.

Usually with a high-end video shoot, you would be in some beautiful studio location with great lighting and expensive cameras on you. The great news is that for an effective online course, you don't need any of that. If you have a modern smartphone, you are 90 percent of the way there. The cameras in today's phones are actually incredibly high quality. Give them good audio and good lighting and no one would know your video was shot on a phone.

For less than one hundred dollars, you can have everything you need to create professional-looking and -sounding video for your online course. Here is a list of all you actually need to pull off a great-looking video on your smartphone:

- simple tripod or microphone stand with a phone grip, approximate cost = $20
- clip-on lavalier microphone that plugs into your smartphone, approximate cost = $25
- LED lighting kit (optional), approximate cost = $50

All you need for a shooting location is your living room or home office. Just make sure your background isn't cluttered or distracting. If you can sit facing a nearby window, then you can go with natural light and skip the LED lighting kit entirely, cutting your cost in half.

The clip-on microphone is key as the audio the phone picks up not only isn't as high quality, but also it's too far away, meaning you'll capture too much room sound and echo, which is unprofessional. Simply having a microphone clipped to your shirt about twelve inches from your face gives you a clean, professional sound.

When it comes time to edit your videos, either to trim off the beginning and end or cut out any mistakes along the way, you can use one of many free video editing platforms. On a Mac, I would recommend the included iMovie software. You can even use iMovie right on your iPhone. If you use Windows, then I would try OpenShot or Movie Maker.

Now that you know how to film talking head–style videos on camera, let's consider an alternative, the slide presentation.

Video Style #2—Slide Presentation or Tutorial

Believe it or not, you don't need to show your face to make an effective online course. Depending on what you are teaching in your videos, a simple slide presentation can work wonderfully. And the good news is, it's even easier and cheaper to pull off than an on-camera, talking head–style shot.

By slide presentation, I mean exactly that. You present a set of slides that you have prepared ahead of time, and you teach the material that way. **This is my favorite style of video for online courses for reasons that I'll address in a moment, and I use it all the time in most of my courses.**

The idea is simple: prepare some slides with text, images, or even embedded video, then record your screen and voice as you click through them and teach the material. Another form of this type of video is an on-screen tutorial where you might be showing a piece of software or clicking through some websites as you explain a concept. This, too, is simply a recording of your computer screen and your voice.

The great news with this type of video is that it can cost you zero to pull off. Here's what you'll need:

- slide-presentation software, such as Google Slides, Apple Keynote, or Microsoft PowerPoint, cost = $0 (for Google Slides)

- screen-recording software, like Loom or ScreenFlow, cost = $0 (for Loom)
- USB microphone to capture your voice (optional), cost = $30

When your slides are prepared, you simply use Loom or ScreenFlow to record everything on your screen, then go full screen with your slides and begin to click through and teach. The software will record both what you see on the screen and your voice, giving you a video you can edit and upload for your course.

Most computers have a decent built-in microphone that you can use for your voice since you'll be relatively close to it when sitting down to film. Alternatively, you can plug in a pair of earbud-style headphones that have a microphone built in. Otherwise, you can spring for an inexpensive USB microphone that sits right in front of you on your desk for more professional-sounding audio.

This style of video is great for content that needs visual aids like images, text, or math to go along with what you're teaching. It's also good for any over-the-shoulder-style videos where you're looking at something on your computer and commenting on it for the student. Like I said, these are my favorite videos to create, and for good reason. Let's break down the pros and cons of both styles.

	Pros	Cons
Talking Head Videos	Visual connection for your student. They can see your face and you can instantly build trust.	Can cost more money because you need more equipment.
	Crucial if teaching something in "real life" like fitness moves, photography, or cooking, for example.	Requires a decent filming space and good lighting.
	Can look high end and professional, making your course subconsciously feel more valuable.	Requires you being on camera, thus your hair or makeup might need to be done.
	Don't require any time preparing slides in advance.	Can seem more formal as you feel all the eyes are on you, which makes some people nervous and tense, leading to an ineffective video.
		Can take longer to film as you will need to reference your notes often.
		Can take longer to edit as you'll have to cut out any time you referenced your notes.

	Pros	Cons
Slide-Presentation Videos	Can be executed with free tools.	Less of a personal connection with the student—they can only hear and not see you.
	No lighting required.	Can seem less professional and subsequently less valuable.
	No beautiful shoot location or decluttering of your house needed.	If there aren't many elements to your slides, it can seem boring for your student to stare at the same slide and listen to you talk.
	No need to do your hair or makeup (or even get dressed, for that matter!).	
	Allows you to read your own notes off your slides, making teaching and presenting much easier.	
	Less pressure to perform because there is no camera on you.	
	Allows you to teach high-level material because you have visual aids supporting your point.	

With all that being said, **I tend to prefer slide-presentation-style videos because I find they are much easier and faster to create**. Even though I have professional cameras, lighting, and a dedicated shooting space, I still prefer to make slides and click through them for most videos. However, there are moments when a talking head–style video is more appropriate, and when that is the case, I won't hesitate to shoot that way.

In fact, **I suggest every online course have at least two talking head videos in them at minimum: the welcome video and the closing-remarks video**. Look your students in the eye and welcome them on camera. It can go a long way toward making them *feel* welcomed and empowered to take your course and get great results. The same is true with a wrap-up or closing-remarks video. Congratulate them for getting all the way to the end and give them final instructions and encouragement as they embark on putting all they've learned into practice.

KAJABI: THE ONLY TOOL YOU NEED TO DELIVER YOUR ONLINE COURSE

So you've researched, outlined, and even filmed your online course. What next? At this point, you need a platform to host and deliver your course to your future customers. The great news is you have lots of wonderful choices here, but I'll make it simple for you: go with Kajabi.

If you remember from the last chapter, I suggested you build your website and do all your email marketing with Kajabi. If you took my advice, then that means you already have the best platform in the world to host and deliver your course. Online courses are Kajabi's bread and butter.

Creating an online course in Kajabi is as simple as uploading your videos, picking a professionally designed theme, adding a description for each video, and clicking Save. It really is that easy. Kajabi even includes what they call "pipelines," which are one-click templates for your course, offer, and sales strategy (more on the selling part in the next chapter).

For the customer experience, your students are able to purchase your course and get immediate digital access to your content through their own private log-in that leads to their own custom product library. This is much like buying e-books through Amazon's Kindle platform. They log in and can see any and every course or digital product they have purchased from you, right there on their computer, tablet, or phone.

The great thing for *you* when you go with Kajabi for hosting your online courses is simplicity. Everything is in one place: your website, email marketing, sales pages, products, and customer-management software. This not only saves you money (not needing to pay for a bunch of separate online tools) but also saves you time and headaches. Just log in to Kajabi and run your business. It's that simple.

WHAT ABOUT MEMBERSHIP SITES?

I've spent this entire chapter talking about online courses. But what if you are interested in selling a membership site? Let's talk.

Membership sites are wonderful products. They give you recurring revenue since customers are signing up for a monthly subscription, they allow you to build a private community where engagement and interaction can be high, and they can be a lot of fun. I've personally built and run three different membership sites over the years, and they've each been a great asset to my business. But I personally don't recommend you *start* your online business with a membership.

Specifically, I recommend you launch a membership only after you launch your first course and after you have at least a thousand people on your email list. Here's why. Online courses give people your core teaching methods in a more straightforward, step-by-step method. This is great when starting out. Also, an online course can be fully automated and hands off for you after you launch it. Membership sites, on the other hand, require ongoing content (more on that in a minute) and engagement.

The reason I would wait to launch a membership until you have at least a thousand people on your email list is because you need a decent amount of people to buy in order to have a valuable community. If you have a list of a thousand people and get a 1 percent conversion rate when selling your membership (which is pretty realistic), that would be ten people. That's the absolute minimum I would want in a community considering most people won't interact, thus making your community pretty empty. Remember that with membership sites, the bigger the community, the more value it offers, and the more interaction your members will get.

The Three Cs of Memberships

If you decide that you're ready to launch a membership site, here is what you need to know. Memberships are built on the three Cs: **content, coaching**, and **community**.

Your content can be a new video uploaded each month or a weekly PDF, or a combination. The idea is that you simply have new content each month to make the membership more valuable. Coaching means live interaction with you, the instructor. Whether through a monthly Zoom webinar, or private YouTube Live session every other week, you should have some live coaching element where you can answer student questions.

And, finally, the third but most critical element is community. Whether in the form of a private Facebook group or a built-in Kajabi Community product (yes, Kajabi has their own community tool baked in, and it's awesome), you must have a place where members can interact, start conversations, and feel connected to each other. Most membership-site owners underestimate the value of the community element and *overestimate* the value of the content. Community is the most important component of a thriving membership, and it is what will keep people from canceling.

Online marketer Ryan Lee once said this about membership sites: "People come for the content, but they stay for the community." I couldn't agree more.

Here's a quick checklist of what you'll want in place when you launch your membership site for the first time:

- a welcome video in the private members' area
- one month's worth of content uploaded and ready
- your community element in place (Kajabi Community or a private Facebook group, for instance)
- a bonus mini course that you can offer as an overdeliver to make that first month feel more substantial
- ideally, a year's worth of monthly content outlined so you know what to create moving forward for the next twelve months

IT'S TIME TO LAUNCH!

After all the hard work of building an online course, you still need to take one more step and actually sell it to your audience. This is usually where people get stuck because they have a bad taste in their mouths when it comes to selling.

In the next chapter, I'm going to show you how to sell with integrity and class, all without feeling salesy or manipulative. I'll walk you through a step-by-step, proven strategy to get your first digital product launched, help a ton of people, and put money in your pocket—even if you've never sold anything in your entire life.

Action Step:

Begin researching what topic you will build your first online course around and start the outlining process. If you haven't already signed up for a free trial of Kajabi, use my link and get an exclusive free mini course: https://www.grahamcochrane.com/kajabi.

Chapter 7

STEP 5: LAUNCH YOUR OFFER

The Art of Selling Without Being Salesy

My first "big boy" full-time job out of college was selling ad spots for a local small-town radio station. My days consisted of wearing an oversized dress shirt and obnoxious tie, sitting in a sad little beige cubicle, and cold-calling local businesses trying to get an appointment with the owner in order to pitch them on radio advertising.

When smiling and dialing didn't work, I was supposed to drive around town and walk right into these establishments to catch the owners or managers off guard and try to pitch them in person. Because, you know, it's harder to hang up on someone who's right in front of you.

I think I threw up a little in my mouth just typing those last two paragraphs. Oh, and in case you were wondering, I only lasted five months in that job. **It turns out I wasn't made for sales. At least, that's what I thought back then.**

Fast-forward just a few short years and I'm now making seven figures a year in my business—by selling. The only difference is this time I'm selling products I really believe in. On top of that, the selling in my business happens through an email and a website, and I'm selling to people who are already interested in what I have to offer.

Sound more appealing to you? I hope so, because in this chapter, I'm going to teach you a method of selling your online courses that not only is effective but also feels authentic and effortless. But before we talk about selling and the art of product launches, it's important that you nail down the price of your online course. This will play a huge role in how much money you can make in your business.

First, I'll explain how to strategically price your products. Then I'll teach you how to write powerful sales copy that still sounds human and approachable. And finally, I'll walk you through the step-by-step process of doing a proper product launch so you sell as many copies as possible.

WHAT SHOULD YOU CHARGE FOR YOUR ONLINE COURSE?

One of the most common questions I get from students is about pricing. This is unsurprising because pricing seems so arbitrary and subjective. Plus, there are many people out there selling online courses at a wide range of prices. The great news is, pricing for online courses does have some rules of thumb. I want to walk you through my simple pricing framework so you know very quickly where you should land with pricing your online course.

My logic with pricing follows something Tim Ferriss wrote a while back that I agree with wholeheartedly: "*I have found that a price range of $50-200 per sale provides the most profit for the least customer service hassle. Price high and then justify.*"

This makes a lot of sense if you think about it. If you sell products for less than fifty dollars, you are likely to attract customers who demand the most but want to pay the least. That has been my experience anyway. In an ideal world, you charge premium prices and only deal with premium customers. But if you charge too much, then you create more potential work for yourself, as premium customers who are spending a lot can require a bit more attention—even if they're nice.

The $50–$200 price range represents that sweet spot: not too low, not too high. It's not so low that you don't make enough per sale. But it's not so high that the customer has to think long and hard about pulling out their credit card and making the purchase.

I've had most of my products fall in this price range over the years, and with great success. My very first online course was called "Pro Tools Boot Camp," and it sold for forty-five dollars. One of my best sellers for the Recording Revolution was called *Rethink Mixing*, and I sold it for ninety-seven dollars. And you know what? That little course has made me over $1 million over a few years' time!

Now, there are a few factors that go into determining your price more specifically, and I have a pricing framework that makes it easy for you.

MY ONLINE-COURSE-PRICING FRAMEWORK

In order to land on your price, you have to determine what level of online course you are selling. Is it a mini course, a flagship online course, or a premium online course? What's the difference? I thought you'd never ask.

- **Mini Courses ($47–$97).** Mini courses are generally defined by length and depth of material. Typically, a mini course is a tightly focused, highly relevant online course that helps your people solve one specific problem or achieve one specific result. These courses are on average two to three hours in length and include at least one downloadable worksheet. They might be made up of eight to ten videos of approximately fifteen minutes in length.
- **Flagship Online Courses ($97–$497).** Flagship courses are likely what comes to mind when you think of an online course. They are fully developed, in-depth training products that give your student a complete end-to-end system for achieving a major milestone or solving a major problem. You will likely build at least one flagship course for your business; it will be a signature product that gets your students great results. It can even be the logical next step after a mini course.

- **Premium Online Course ($497–$1,997).** Courses can deliver
  an even more premium experience to your customers by adding
  more than just video content. Coaching elements like live calls, a
  private community with access to you, or custom feedback can all
  raise the value of the course significantly. Typically, at this price
  point, you need to sell with a live webinar.

Why do I end my prices with the number seven, you might ask?
There were some pricing psychology studies done in the '70s and '80s
that suggested prices ending in a seven or nine performed better than the
rounded-up number. For example, a product priced at $97 would sell more
copies than if it were priced at $100. Since then, however, there have been
other studies to disprove that theory.

So why do I keep using sevens? Because I like the way it looks. Go
figure.

So ask yourself, *Which of these three types of courses am I building?*
Then pick a price in that range that feels good to you. A few more things to
note about pricing before we move on:

- **You can typically charge more if the student can make money
  from your course.** This makes sense if you think about it. I
  charge more for a course on starting an online business than I do
  for a course on recording guitar.
- **The tighter the niche, the more you can charge.** If you are
  one of the only people in the world offering a course on
  English pronunciation for native Japanese speakers who are in
  international business (like one of my students), then you can
  charge more than someone just teaching people how to speak
  English in general.
- **Keep in mind it's easier to raise prices later than it is to drop
  them.** If you're in doubt about what price to go with in your
  suggested range, start on the lower side. You can always increase
  it later. Your early adopters will have been rewarded.

What if I told you there was a way to increase revenue (and profit) when selling your online course without having to actually raise the price? Would you be interested?

HOW TO INCREASE REVENUE 50 PERCENT WITHOUT LIFTING A FINGER

I want to share a powerful secret with you. In reality, it's not much of a secret to most smart businesses and brands around the world. And it's not hidden from you, the consumer, at all. In fact, it's a secret that's hidden in plain sight. Do you know what it is?

OK, I'll tell you: when it comes to product pricing, there is no one-size-fits-all scenario. **Some people will be glad to spend more with you if you only offered more value.** Give people the option to give you more money.

If you have only one tier or option for your online course at one price, you're making a mistake. When done right, tiered pricing can easily increase your average purchase price by 25–50 percent—all without lifting a finger. And like I said, most smart brands are doing this. Let's cover some examples of tiered pricing you might already be familiar with.

- **Coffee shops.** When you walk into your favorite coffee shop and order a cup of regular coffee, what follow-up question does the barista usually ask? "What size would you like?" Because, of course, not everyone wants the same amount of coffee. Some will spend two dollars for a twelve-ounce cup, and others will spend four dollars on a twenty-two-ounce cup. This is tiered pricing at its most basic.
- **Smartphones.** When you're ready to buy the latest iPhone (or Android—I still love you), you realize that there isn't just one version of the iPhone for sale. There is a basic and a pro. There are three different phone and screen sizes. You can even pay more for extra internal storage. I might go in and spend $499 on a mini

iPhone, and you might walk out having spent over $1,000 on the biggest one they have. Tiered pricing.

- **New cars.** New automobiles offer another classic example of tiered pricing. When you go to your local dealership or look online, you'll notice that deciding which car to buy is just the beginning. Your next decision is which trim level to buy. For example, a base-model Honda Pilot LX might cost $31,000 while the top-of-the-line Elite trim with more technology, convenience features, and sport appearance will run you $48,000. Yet more tiered pricing.

Everyone has a different amount they're willing to spend, and there's always someone out there who wants the best you have to offer. It reminds me of something someone told me years ago that I will never forget.

I was working as an audio engineer for a cool software company, doing voice-over work. One day after recording all morning with the voice-over talent, we took a lunch break and proceeded to talk about gear. The talent asked me if I preferred PCs or Macs for recording. I told him I was a Mac guy, and instantly, a bond was formed. Turns out he not only loves Apple products as well, but he is their ideal customer. I know this because he said something that at the time blew my mind, but now makes so much sense.

"Graham," he said in his low, booming voice, "I always buy the most expensive Mac."

Wait, what?

Yeah, on principle, this guy buys the most fully loaded Mac that Apple will offer him. Simply because he wants the best. Fascinating. At the time, I was making only $30,000 a year as a lowly audio engineer so I thought he was crazy. Now I see that what's actually crazy is to not believe that people like this guy exist.

I just did a quick glance on the Apple Store right now to see what tiered pricing they offer for their best-selling iMac computer, and here's what I found. I can grab a base-model iMac for $1,099. But if I spring for the bigger screen, faster processor, most RAM, and biggest hard drives, I can rack up a bill of over $5,000. Actually, $5,428 to be exact.

That's five times the cost of the base-model iMac. And that's a ton of money Apple would have missed out on with that voice-over guy if they didn't offer all those upgrades. Tiered pricing works!

So how can you take advantage of tiered pricing yourself? Here's what you need to do with your online course:

- **Offer two to three options.** One will be the basic or core version of the course. The upper tier(s) will come bundled with more goodies. Any more than three options and you lose or confuse people.
- **Charge 50–100 percent more for upper-tier courses.** To make this work, you want to have a clear distinction between the options. Don't nickel-and-dime people for marginal gains. Take your base price for the course and make the next version either 50 percent more or twice as much.
- **Add value that doesn't cost you.** There are lots of ways to create a more premium version that doesn't cut into your bottom line. For example, you could add additional digital downloads or bonus video modules, ongoing support via email or a community, or access to you via scalable coaching.

Remember that course I mentioned earlier, *Rethink Mixing*, that made me over a million dollars? For three years I sold it at only one price: $99. After learning about tiered pricing, I decided to put it to work with that course as a test.

I created two additional tiers, priced at $149 and $349, accordingly. The middle tier included the course plus two additional downloads and a custom song critique from me via a onetime email exchange. Total time involved for me to fulfill this critique: five minutes. And get this: most people who purchased that tier never even cashed in on their song critique. I called this version the *Rethink Mixing PLUS Bundle*. The $349 option included everything in the $149 version but added a one-hour video call with me. I called this the *Rethink Mixing ELITE Bundle*.

Now, some people did go for the $349 version, which was great. But most went for the first two tiers. Here's the crazy thing though: over 50 percent of customers chose the middle tier at $149. **That means by simply having that option available, I made 25 percent more money overall.**

Imagine if you had two tiers of your course, one for $97 and the other for $197. If half of your people spring for the $197 option, you'll have increased your revenue by 50 percent without having to do anything. That's the power of tiered pricing.

THE PSYCHOLOGY OF TIERED PRICING

There's powerful psychology happening with tiered pricing that most people seem to miss. When you offer multiple tiers of your product, you shift the question in your customer's mind from "Should I buy this?" to "Which *one* should I buy?"

Subtly and subconsciously, by offering even just one additional option to your prospect on your sales page, you stop them from deciding whether or not to buy and instead prime them to figure out which option would be a good fit for them if they *were* to buy. This gets them imagining future use of the product, which only helps them build desire for it.

It's simple, elegant, subtle, and powerful.

So, back to your course, I want you to create a slightly more expensive version of it. Think about what ways you could add more value to it that don't take too much money or effort, but still allow you to charge 50–100 percent more for it. You'll then be primed to make more on average for every sale, all while still being able to offer a price you feel comfortable with.

SALES-COPY FEARS

Now that you've priced out your course, it's time to sell it. And the way you sell online is through writing powerful sales copy (words) that communicates the value of the product and makes a compelling offer to the prospect. In just a moment, I'm going to give you a step-by-step, proven formula for writing powerful, effective sales copy for your online course, but before I do that I want to address the elephant in the room: your fear.

People get scared and overwhelmed when it comes to selling. Specifically, when it comes to writing sales copy for their online courses, they freeze. Here are some common fears I hear:

- "Selling makes me feel pushy or manipulative."
- "Sales copy seems complicated."
- "I'm not a good writer or communicator."
- "I'm afraid of being too long (or too short) with my sales copy."
- "I just don't know where to start!"

These fears and concerns are natural. Most of us aren't born salespeople, and on top of that, sales (or selling) seems to get a bad rap these days. It seems sleazy, scammy, or manipulative. Like you're forcing someone to part with their money. But that's simply because of years and years of exposure to bad sales tactics, tactics that truthfully are as ineffective as they are icky feeling for both the customer and salesperson.

Selling doesn't have to be this way. **In fact, the best sales experience is an enjoyable one for both parties. One in which the customer *wants* to part with his money.** And, even better, selling can happen online now instead of face-to-face. This takes the pressure off *you* and makes the customer feel like he or she is *choosing* to buy rather than being sold to.

Did you know that we actually get the word *sell* from the Old English word *sellan*, which means "to give"? How enlightening is that? **Ethical selling is simply giving people what they want and need.**

Building things people want and then offering them up in exchange for a fair amount of money is all I've been doing over the years. I've never forced, coerced, or manipulated someone into buying anything. People are going to buy what they want to buy. That being said, there's a method to strategically positioning what you're offering as appealing and accurately communicating the value of your course. That's where smart sales copy comes into play.

THE THREE-STEP SALES-COPY FORMULA

Writing powerful sales copy is truly an art form. It can take years to master, but the payoff is worth it. There's a reason why the world's top copywriters can command over $100,000 to write a simple sales page, because the words they use can create a flood of orders coming in for their clients.

I don't propose to be an expert copywriter, and I'm certainly always learning. But I have figured out a few tried-and-true things that work each and every time, and as someone who thrives on simplicity, I've boiled everything I've learned down into a three-step formula.

Much of what I'm about to teach you is a blend of techniques I learned from legends like Ray Edwards, Jay Abraham, and Ramit Sethi. If you want to dive even deeper than I have here, I would highly suggest reading any material written by those gentlemen.

No matter what you intend to sell, this three-step formula will help you sell lots of it. How do I know? Because it's designed to speak to humans as they are, not as we wish they were.

These three steps can be remembered by three letters: PSA. Like a public service announcement, your PSA sales-copy formula will accurately announce your product's value and attract the right buyers every time. Here's what the letters stand for:

- P = person/problem/pain
- S = story/struggle/solution
- A = ask for the sale

Each letter represents a step in the formula. Each sales page (or sales video) should cover all three steps, in order. The actual copy (or words) you choose can and should be wildly different from mine, but the elements are the same. Let me walk you through them in depth now and offer examples.

Step 1—Person, Problem, Pain

The very first part of your sales page (or video or email) should address the *P* in the formula. This step is all about three things:

- What **person** is this product for?
- What **problem** does it solve?
- What **pain** is this person going through?

As simple as those three questions are, you'd be surprised how often people skip right past them when writing sales copy and instead start talking about their course and how amazing it is.

Friend, no one will care about your online course unless they know that it's for them and can address their pain point. Remember, we're talking to real humans. So *talk to them* before you talk about what you want to *sell to them*.

In a practical sense, when someone lands on your sales page for your course, you have only a few seconds to grab their attention. Naturally, they are skimming the page to know if they are in the right place. *Is this for me?* is what they are subconsciously asking. Your job is to answer that right away, without delay, in order to keep them lingering a few moments longer to see what you have to say.

Here is an example from the top of one of my sales pages for a membership site I run:

If you are a business owner who is already making a few hundred to a few thousand dollars a month and would like to cross over that $100,000 a year mark, then I've got something special for you today. But first let me ask you this—have you ever wondered why some people seem to easily create six-figure incomes online and others just struggle?

Do you notice how I address the three Ps of this first step of the formula?

- Person = online business owner making less than $100,000 a year
- Problem = want to make over $100,000 a year

- Pain = frustration that other business owners seem to scale easily while they struggle

This step usually is just a sentence or two, but don't underestimate this step because of its simplicity or brevity. Addressing the three Ps here is critical because it immediately helps qualify your prospect as the right kind of lead (or not) and shows that you understand who they are and what they want or need. Without this, the rest of the sales page is pointless.

Step 2—Story, Struggle, Solution

The second letter in the PSA sales page is S, and this has everything to do with connection. If we've identified who this product is for and what it helps them do in the first step, then here we want to go deeper and connect with them in a human way. The S in this step of the formula is all about three things:

- sharing a relatable **story** of your own **struggle** with the same problem you just mentioned
- highlighting the desired outcome that you (and your prospect) had in light of that **struggle**
- revealing what **solution** you discovered and how it can help your prospect as well

There is power in storytelling. Comedians know this, Jesus of Nazareth knew this, and good salespeople know this. Stories make us human and allow us to connect. And that, my friend, is what's missing from most bad sales copy I see: human connection.

Something happens when good people go to write the sales copy for their online course. They become robots. It's as if all heart, emotion, and humanity are replaced with robotic, corporate-marketing speak that means absolutely nothing—both to them and their prospects.

Why do we do this? Because we freeze up. We don't know what to say, so we say whatever sounds professional. No bueno. As copywriters, what we want to do immediately after identifying who this course is for and what pain or problem it's going to solve is talk to them human to human. **Tell them a story that shows you understand their pain and can empathize with it. Show them that you've been where they are and struggled with the same things. But don't end there. Like all good stories, you have a happy ending—the solution.** Which, of course, is your product.

Here's an example from that same sales page as before:

> *I spent the first eighteen months of my online business journey on government assistance in the form of food stamps, making little to no money and questioning every minute of my "decision" to remain self-employed. But two things began to happen to me in years three and four of my business that changed everything: I invested in coaching, and I started to build out a clear growth path for my customers.*

Do you see how I'm being human here? I'm sharing my own personal story of struggle with business, including my internal fears and insecurities. But then I go on to explain how I began to find a solution.

Your story might be long, or it might be short. It might have a lot of detail, or it might just give some detail. **What matters is that you share *your* story. That is all.** You can't share what you haven't experienced, so don't try. Just be you. Imperfect, human you. People can tell when you're being real, and it goes a long way to establishing a connection that will make them feel more comfortable spending money with you.

If you've done your job well addressing the person/problem/pain and told a compelling and relatable story of your similar struggle, then transitioning to your product as the solution is easy. It only takes five words: "So that's why I created . . ."

No need to make it any fancier than that. You know their pain, you've been there before, you were tired of the struggle, and you found an answer and packaged it up into a solution, which is your product. Your story of struggle is what led you to create your course so that others won't struggle with the same thing. This message is simple, elegant, and powerful.

How to Sell Your Solution

Let's briefly pause here in the formula so I can give you some specific tips on actually selling your solution in your sales copy. There are five common elements I include here that are pretty straightforward and don't involve much (if any) creativity.

- **Benefit Bullets.** Create ten to fifteen benefit-driven bullet points about what they will learn in the course. These should be benefits, not features. A good example would be, "You'll learn how to play your favorite songs on guitar, without needing to ever read sheet music." A bad example would be, "This course features eight-plus hours of HD video content." Nobody cares about features. They care about benefits—what results they'll see after taking your course.

- **Price Anchoring.** When it comes to revealing the price of your course, you want to communicate how much of a value it is. We do this by anchoring your price as compared to more expensive alternate solutions. Be sure to address those alternatives in your sales copy and show how much they cost. Your course will look like a bargain in comparison. For example, I always compare my music-recording courses ($99–$299) to the cost of an audio degree ($25,000+).

- **The Guarantee.** Something I learned from Jay Abraham years ago was just how important your money-back guarantee is. Buying a course online is risky to the customer. What if the course doesn't work for them? What if they aren't happy with it? At that point, their money is gone. Your job as the business owner is to *transfer that risk* from the customer to you. Tell them they can refund their purchase within 30 days (or 60 or 365 days) if they aren't happy for any reason. This one simple section of your sales page will put them at ease and give you more sales than almost anything else. Refunds are a natural part of business, and online courses are no exception. The extra sales that come from having such a strong guarantee will likely outweigh any potential refunds.

- **FAQ.** Most people have questions when buying something. And most people's questions will be roughly the same. So go ahead and address those common questions head-on with an honest and straightforward FAQ (frequently asked questions) section. This can help overcome most common objections.
- **Testimonials.** If you have any compelling testimonials from previous customers, be sure to sprinkle them throughout your sales page. If you are launching a new (or your first) online course and have no testimonials, then simply get some from students who have gotten great results with your free content. Testimonials allow your prospect not to just take *your* word for it, but to see that others think your material is amazing.

I recommend putting these elements in this order at this point of the sales page. The only exception is with the testimonials, which, depending on how many you have, can and should be spread all around the sales page. Again, these elements are pretty straightforward, and after you've included them, you're almost done. There's just one final step in the three-part formula.

Step 3—Ask for the Sale

Finally, we come to the step in the sales-copy formula where you need to literally ask them to buy your product. We call this "asking for the sale."

Going back to my radio advertising sales days, one of the *only* things I remember from my training was to "ask for the sale!" And my manager made a really big deal about it. This honestly confused me because I thought that would be an obvious part of selling—asking people to buy your thing. But it turns out this is the one step most people too easily assume is obvious that they don't explicitly do it.

Here's what you do: **Tell your prospect exactly what you want them to do.** Most sales pages will look like some variation of "Click the button below to join now!" It's that simple. This is also where you can and should give any details necessary about what they should expect when they sign up.

Back to my membership-site example. Here's what I put:

If you join this week before membership closes, you can get access to all this coaching for just $97/mo. So lock in this crazy low price before enrollment closes. Just click the button below to join, and after a simple checkout process, you'll be taken instantly to the members' area where you can begin diving into the content and community!

Remember: you can't make them buy, but you must *ask* them to buy, and you must believe in your heart that it's a smart choice for them.

There you have it: the simple three-step sales-copy formula that I and many other online entrepreneurs have used to sell millions of dollars' worth of product. Just follow the PSA outline and you'll be sure to hit the key elements of effective sales copy. Will your first sales page be your best? Nope. But can it get the job done? You better believe it. Stick to the formula, be human, and you'll do just fine.

BUILDING YOUR SALES PAGE

Before you can sell your course, you will need a sales page—a place online you can point your audience to so they can find out more about your course and actually purchase it if it's a good fit for them.

After you've finalized your sales copy, you can quickly and easily build a beautiful sales page using a tool like Kajabi. Start with one of their predesigned templates or build it from scratch with their drag-and-drop elements, including text, images, and video. At this point, you are simply formatting your words so they're readable and appealing. Don't go crazy here. When in doubt, keep it visually simple. Remember that the words you say are what matters most when selling, not how they're formatted.

One final note on sales pages before we move on to your launch strategy. **Whether you choose to use a sales video at the top or not, either way I'd recommend you have a full-text version of your sales copy written out.** As effective as videos can be for selling, they aren't skimmable. Some people don't want to watch a video. They simply want to skim or read your page and decide for themselves if what you're selling is right for them. Give them that option by including the actual copy written out on your sales page.

IT'S TIME TO LAUNCH YOUR COURSE!

So you've built your course, and you've written the sales copy for your first sales page. Now it's time to do a proper product launch to your email list. Product launches are a great way to build excitement with your audience, help a ton of people, and put a pile of cash in your bank account in a short amount of time. Now I'll outline a step-by-step model you can follow to launch your first (or next) product and make it as profitable as possible.

Step 1—The Pre-Launch (Week Before)

The first thing you must realize is that if you simply tell everyone that your course is for sale, you won't be as successful as you could be. You'd think launching would be that simple, but it's not. The key to having a successful launch of anything is to build excitement *beforehand*.

Everyone who has ever successfully launched something knows this. From Apple, to movie executives, to popular bands and artists, the strategy is the same: **create hype in advance of the product launch**.

Every time Apple releases a new model of the iPhone, they host a big live event and unveil their latest smartphone in all its glory weeks in advance of its release date. Movie studios release trailers of their films months before they screen in theaters (or stream online). And musicians always release a single long before their new album is available in order to gain fans and whet listeners' appetites for more. We want to do the exact same thing when it comes to launching our online courses.

One of the truly good guys online and a pioneer in knowledge commerce, Jeff Walker has popularized his product-launch formula, and it works like a charm. He wrote an entire book on the subject called *Launch*, and it's fantastic.

What Jeff teaches is to create three pre-launch videos that go live the week before you actually intend to launch your course. These pieces of content will line up with the core subject matter of your course and build anticipation. These will be free videos that you drop one at a time, and will accomplish three important things:

1. **Get results for your audience and establish credibility.** No fluff or teaser stuff here.
2. **Hint that something big is coming.** Each piece will hint at the next one, leading to the eventual hint that a product is coming next week.
3. **Create engagement and discussion with your audience around the free content.** This interaction with your audience all week long helps build the anticipation and get them excited.

While there are a lot of ways you can go about creating your three pre-launch videos, here is a template that might get your wheels turning. Again, consider this a jumping-off point. Anything really works for pre-launch content as long as it accomplishes the three objectives above.

Video 1—Counterintuitive Angle (10-25 min)
Share a counterintuitive or unique angle in this first video. You want to grab their attention at the beginning with a unique twist that will make them curious. Much like the "story of struggle" element in your sales copy, have an "I was just like you" moment where you identify with where they are. This struggle could be either yours or that of a client of yours.

Then reveal three big secrets or tips that they could use to see results or eliminate that pain. You want to give them three really helpful insights or secrets that will give them those sacred aha moments. Finally, leave them with a taste of what's coming in the next video. This will build more anticipation.

Video 2—The One Strategy (10-25 min)
In this second video, you want to go big and teach them one thing in depth. Pick one strategy or technique you can cover comprehensively in a

simple video. Be generous here and blow their minds with one of your best strategies.

The best techniques to teach here are the ones that are the quickest and easiest to implement as a student. That way they get instant results and are even more sold on what you have to offer. Don't skimp out on this video. Share something so good and helpful that it causes them to wonder just how good your paid stuff must be if this is what you're giving out for free.

Video 3—The Case Study (10–25 min)

For the final pre-launch video, I would feature one of your students or clients who you've helped get the desired result that your audience wants. This could be from previous consulting work, a student who applied some of your free material to great results, or a test group of a handful of people who you gave free or discounted access to the course beforehand in exchange for feedback and testimonials. Film a short interview with them or solicit a powerful testimonial.

Announce you've put together a complete system. At the end of the video, tell them that you've got a whole system that will help *them* get the same results as your featured case study and you'll share more in the next video.

Final thought on these pre-launch videos: ideally, these videos will be private, meaning they aren't just uploaded to YouTube or your website for anyone to see. They should only be available to people on your email list. Or if you want to promote them publicly on social media or on YouTube, then make people opt in to your list to view them. That way you keep the videos private and build your list at the same time.

Step 2—Launch Week

After building a buzz during your pre-launch week, it's time to actually launch your product and let people buy. But how you do this is critical. There are three key components to a successful course launch:

1. Daily emails

2. Scarcity or urgency
3. An onboarding sequence for new customers

Let's start with the emails. Most people feel like emailing every day during a launch is bugging or annoying their people. This is simply their insecurity creeping up, and it's not true. If people are irritated, they can unsubscribe from your list at any point. They wouldn't buy from you anyway. Remember: you're not trying to make friends; you're trying to run a business.

Launch Week Emails

Now here's what you do. Starting on Monday and ending on Friday, email your list each day and cover a different angle each time. Email two to three times on the last day (Friday) for that final push.

Why so many emails? First, most people don't check their inboxes every day. Second, even if they do check every day, they might miss your email. Third, not every angle or email will connect with everyone on your list. And fourth, people procrastinate and need to hear an offer multiple times before taking action, especially if there is scarcity involved (more on that in a moment). Here's a template you can use for your launch week emails that will work wonders.

- **Day 1 (Monday):** Announce the product is for sale and mention the scarcity element (more on this in a minute).
- **Day 2 (Tuesday):** Mention one of the bonuses that they get for joining.
- **Day 3 (Wednesday):** Feature a testimonial from a new or previous customer. Remind them of the scarcity element.
- **Day 4 (Thursday):** Feature some FAQs about the product to encourage those on the fence to buy—and buy now!
- **Day 5 (Friday a.m.), Email 1:** Tell them this is their last chance. The launch week opportunity ends tonight at midnight.
- **Day 5 (Friday p.m.), Email 2:** Offer a quick reminder that the launch offer goes away in a few hours, and mention the bonuses they get for joining.

- **Day 5 (Friday 10 p.m.), Email 3:** This should be a very simple "You have a couple hours left"–type email.

When sending these emails, be sure to set your email client (Kajabi, for example) to exclude people on your list who have already purchased that product. That way someone who buys your course will no longer receive any remaining launch emails.

Build In Scarcity

Key to this launch working is this scarcity or urgency element I've been mentioning. **Let me be clear about this: building scarcity into your launch is *critical* if you want to drive sales.**

People put off till tomorrow what they could do today, unless there really is no opportunity to do it tomorrow. Then they are compelled to decide to take action or not. That's what we want to accomplish by adding scarcity to your launch. Here are three classic ways to do so:

- **Close the Cart.** Tell them the product will no longer be for sale after Friday at midnight (or whenever your launch week ends). This works super well, but it's not my favorite strategy because I like evergreen automated funnels (which we will cover in the next chapter).
- **Price Goes Up.** Tell them the lower launch week price only lasts until Friday at midnight when it'll go up to the normal price. If they want it at this great price, now is the time to act.
- **Limited Time Bonuses.** Create and offer one or two really incredible bonuses that they'll get if they buy during launch week. These have to be super desirable, but the draw of wanting those bonuses for free works super well. Again, with this model they can still buy the course next week, but the bonuses won't be included anymore.

While I said closing the cart isn't my favorite option, it is the most effective one. And honestly, if you're just starting out, it might be best to close the cart after your first launch so you can generate as many sales as possible, evaluate your sales page and launch emails, and then decide to automate your course in the future (which we'll cover in the next chapter).

You want to build in scarcity and email three times on the last day because people procrastinate. These final three emails are so important because typically half of your launch week sales will come on that final day.

Include an Onboarding Email Sequence

Finally, before you launch, you will want to have a simple, prewritten welcome email sequence that will go out automatically to all new customers of your course. This can be a simple three- to seven-day series of emails that help guide new students through the course, giving them one simple Action Step each day to better dive in and take advantage of all your course has to offer.

This email sequence accomplishes two things: (1) it makes people feel welcome and excited to watch your videos, and (2) it generally reduces refund requests. Students who don't just buy the course but actually watch the videos and take action tend to get results. And students who get results are more satisfied with their purchase and won't ask for a refund.

These do not need to be intricate emails. Just think through the three to seven things about the course you want them to check out and write a simple email for each one. Have a welcome email be sent out immediately upon purchase and then a new one each day after that for three to seven days. That's it. This can all be automated in Kajabi.

How Much Should You Expect to Make?

Let me address the question that I think is not addressed often enough or with ample clarity. When launching a product, you need to have a revenue goal in mind. Otherwise, you won't know if the launch was successful or not. But here's the problem: most people just make up a number that they *hope* to make or *think* they will make. But that number isn't based on anything other than a guess or a feeling.

Even if your product is good, your copy is good, and your launch is good, most people on your email list won't actually buy your course. Not even half of your people. I hate to be the one to tell you this, but your realistic benchmark for a launch should be 0.5 to 1 percent of your email list.

Sound low? That's because it is. That's the reality of most solid launches. Can you do better than that? Sure. Can you do worse? Of course. Everyone's results will vary. But after doing this for years and seeing industry-standard numbers, I can tell you this is a great realistic goal for any launch you do. Let's break down the math.

Launch Math Example 1
- Email List—10,000
- Product Price—$97
- Target Sales = 50–100
- **Target Launch Revenue = $4,850–$9,700**

Launch Math Example 2
- Email List—5,000
- Product Price—$297
- Target Sales = 25–50
- **Target Launch Revenue = $7,425–$14,850**

You can see how, in the second example, the person has half the list size as the first person, but their course sells for three times the price. This gives them similar potential launch revenue on the low end and higher launch revenue on the high end. **It's all about list size and product price. Those are your two factors that make the difference.**

One of my clients had a course that made $20,000 on launch week, and she was discouraged. This was before she met me. It turns out she had spent $20,000 to film and promote the course. She had done all that work to make literally no money. In talking to her, I learned that $20,000 was actually a really good launch for her email list size. She was shocked. Had she known that $20,000 was what she was likely to earn, she would have never spent that much to film and advertise it.

Remember the rule: expect to sell 0.5 to 1 percent of your total email list—and mentally prepare accordingly. How big is your email list at launch? With this rule, how many copies sold should be your low-end goal? How much does your course cost? Multiply those two numbers for your low-end launch-revenue goal and then get out there and crush it.

SOME FINAL THOUGHTS

As we wrap up this chapter, I want to give you a few final thoughts on product launches:

- **You're not annoying your list.** Yes, you will be sending out a ton of emails over the course of two weeks, but one week of that is amazing *free* content, and the other week is a huge announcement week that won't ever happen again. If people don't like it, then they aren't your ideal subscribers anyway, and they can excuse themselves from your list.
- **Stick to your deadline.** If you say the offer goes away at midnight on Friday, it better go away. People will learn to respect that you mean what you say and it's not just manipulation. You have to back up real scarcity by honoring what you said.
- **Check in with your first few customers.** Email (or better yet, call) your first five to ten customers on launch day to thank them and make sure the entire process went smoothly for them. This will help you catch any technical issues with the course and will also create some superfans.
- **Resume your normal content.** The week after launch week, get right back to normal, free, amazing content going out in emails, as if nothing ever happened. This trains your people to know that when you do a launch, you go all out, and then it's over. They don't have to worry about constant promotion, and they can appreciate when you *do* promote in the future.

And that's really it. Launching for the first time can be scary. And honestly, *every* launch feels like a lot of work. But it's worth it, and if you follow the formula I just gave you, it will work for you. The great news is you don't have to launch all the time to make a good living. In fact, I don't recommend it.

LET'S AUTOMATE YOUR BUSINESS!

In the next chapter, I want to get to my absolute favorite part of this entire business model, making it automatic. Using the same tools you already have in place at this point, by simply automating the lead-qualifying and sales process of your digital products, you can start to increase revenue all while working less. This is when online business gets fun and you can maintain a great lifestyle while benefiting from the flexibility and freedom it affords you.

This is what has allowed my business to grow all while working less and enjoying life more. If that sounds appealing to you, then keep on reading because that, my friend, is what we are ready to cover next.

Action Step:

Mark a date on your calendar for your first product-launch week. Then work backward and outline the steps you'll need to take to create the launch, pre-launch, sales copy, and product pricing. Finally, take that first step this week.

Chapter 8

STEP 6: AUTOMATE YOUR SYSTEM

Turn Your Products into a Passive-Income Stream

As I write this chapter, it's 9:53 on a Tuesday morning. Earlier today, I woke up around five thirty, made a cup of fresh coffee, and read my Bible for about forty-five minutes while the house was still quiet. Then I woke my daughters and made them breakfast. After helping them and my wife get out the door for school and work on time, I went to the gym for an intense hour-long workout, followed by a hot shower and a hot breakfast of my own. Now I'm sitting at my kitchen island with my laptop and my second cup of coffee.

After writing for a few hours, I'll probably go get a haircut at my local barbershop, swing by Costco to pick up some sparkling waters, and then catch up with my family when they get home around four. **Technically, I won't have done any work for my businesses today, and yet I'll make somewhere just north of $5,000 just the same!** And another $5,000 tomorrow, and the next day, and so on.

In a given week, I only put in about eight hours of actual work, but my businesses both pay me handsomely. How does this happen? And more importantly, why am I sharing this with you?

This, my friend, is what I love to talk about the most, and it's the absolute best reason to own an online business. **Getting paid to share what you know is incredible, but getting paid whether you work or not is even better.**

Here's the formula for my work-less, earn-more lifestyle: my content gets me discovered, my lead magnets draw people onto my list, and my automated email funnel offers my products. It's that simple. And it's totally possible for you to do the exact same thing.

IS PASSIVE INCOME A MYTH?

You see, all the work you've done up to this point is what can help you create passive income. Oops, I said it. *Passive income.* The phrase that either makes people skeptical or angry (or both). People seem to hate the term *passive income.* And for good reason.

It's thrown around a lot and abused by online business gurus who want to lure you into buying their pointless coaching package and then leave you with nothing truly helpful or actionable. The idea of making gobs of money and then lounging in a hammock on the beach is dangled in front of us so often these days that it starts to all sound like some slimy Ponzi scheme. You remember what your parents told you growing up, right? If it sounds too good to be true, it probably is.

I have to be honest: passive income is one of those topics that I love and hate. I love it because it's absolutely real. I hate it because when I talk about it, I get compared to those slimeballs who make a bad name for our industry. But I press on and share this material because it is life changing.

Passive income is what has allowed me to be a more present husband and father. It's allowed me to have time to exercise and get enough sleep. It's allowed me to live in the South of France with my family for a month, and disappear to the Rocky Mountains of Colorado for two weeks—without needing to work. And still make money!

Yes, passive income is very real. And there are many ways to create it. What you've built so far has laid the foundation for you to create your *own* passive-income stream. You just need this final step.

THE #HUSTLE CULTURE

There is another reason passive income is viewed so negatively for some. There is a cultural issue here, at least in the United States, that has shaped the way people see the world. We elevate people who work hard. We celebrate the #hustle on Instagram. We admire people who forsake everything else and grind it out for success and wealth. We've glorified workaholism by giving it better PR.

So when people like me talk about "passive" income, it seems to signify "lazy" income. As if I don't believe in hard work, or that I just want something for nothing. But you and I both know that you can't get something for nothing. And you've seen how much work it has taken up to this point to build your online business.

No, I'm not lazy. The opposite of hustle isn't laziness—it's diligence. Merriam-Webster's dictionary defines *diligence* as "steady, earnest, and energetic effort." That's exactly what I've been doing for almost a decade and a half now. I believe that steady, earnest effort on the *right* things can lead to great rewards.

Working smarter, not harder, should actually be the more esteemed method. It doesn't take any strategy or intelligence to just work all the time. Plus, where's the fun in that? It takes *way* more creativity and diligence to stop doing #AllTheThings, evaluate what activities in your business actually lead to more consistent sales, and then do only those things. So that's what I do. And it turns out it's a lot easier than most think to grow your income while working less.

AUTOMATION IS THE KEY

Sure, having no money is bad. But having money and no time to enjoy it isn't much better. **Having money *and* time is the key, and automation is the way to have both because it buys back your time and gives you freedom.** Passive doesn't mean you won't have to work. Rather, it means you do a *fixed* amount of work and earn disproportionate (or scalable) income.

Another term for what we're doing here is creating an evergreen business—one that puts money in our pockets all day, every day, whether we are working in it or not. **This evergreen, automated style of business is what's allowing me to write this book for you right now.** Because I have cash coming in whether I work or not, I can afford to do things I'm passionate about, like writing a book, even without a promise of it ever paying me a dime.

Whether you want to free up your time, scale up your income, or both, the key is automation. And the automation tool of choice for us is email marketing. Using the same software you already have in place (Kajabi, Mailchimp, ConvertKit, etc.), you're going to set up what I call an automated money machine.

YOUR AUTOMATED MONEY MACHINE

Let me tell you a little marketing secret: *The best people to sell to are those who have just found you and are most interested in you right now*. Please read that last sentence again. If you can understand the simple wisdom of that truth, then you will understand why what I'm about to teach you works so well.

If it's true that the best people to sell to are those who have just found you and are most interested in you right now, then the key to your prosperity is to create an email sequence that sells to them for you—automatically! Think of it as an automated launch sequence only for new people, and it's completely hands off.

Some call this email sequence a "funnel." You might hear the term "evergreen funnel" or "email autoresponder," and it all means the same thing. It's a set of prewritten emails that all of your new email subscribers receive automatically that introduces them to your online course. This email funnel is the missing ingredient that can take a launch-only online business and turn it into a truly passive-income business. And it's worth it. Here's how it works.

- **Write five to seven days' worth of emails.** These will go out each day, starting the first day after your new email subscriber downloads your lead magnet. Kajabi or any of the email marketing platforms can easily trigger automated email sequences for people who opt in to your list.
- **Overdeliver with super valuable content.** In these emails, you will teach something to subscribers or give them something relevant to your lead magnet or site and make it *so* valuable they feel glad they joined your list. Remember the value circle from chapter 2. At this point, they will have received at least three pieces of valuable content from you, and you will have built a ton of trust, credibility, and goodwill.
- **Transition to an offer during the final three days.** Pivot from the content to a relevant product that would be a natural no-brainer for them if they've liked the previous few days' worth of emails.

Here's an example of a five-day email sequence that has worked wonders for me over the years and has generated hundreds of thousands of dollars.

Day 1—Teach Something Valuable

The goal of this first email is twofold: to inform them that you will be sending them some of your best tips over the next few days (this creates anticipation) and to actually teach them something helpful and actionable right away.

This email sets the tone for the relationship by showing them you are all about giving value and not wasting their time. Make them happy they opened the email and then promise more where that came from. End the email with a simple PS that primes them to look for tomorrow's email with another powerful tip.

Day 2—Share a Powerful Insight

In this email, I like to teach a powerful but counterintuitive insight that makes the subscriber question prevailing wisdom in my niche while simultaneously building credibility for my own knowledge and experience. This can be done with a simple story of what you *used* to believe about something and how that all changed once you *discovered* this new insight.

If the insight can be applied right away, even better. But the point here on day two is again to add immense value, make the subscriber feel glad that they opened the email, and to build anticipation for tomorrow's email. You are subtly training them to look for and open your emails. This is a good thing.

Day 3—Transition into Product

This is probably the most important email of the five, and it doesn't have to be that hard to write either. The subject line (and first half of the email) should still be all about teaching something powerful. Share another insight, discovery, or truth you've come to believe over the years and make it valuable for the reader.

Halfway through the email is when you transition to your product. This can be very similar language to your sales page when you transition from your discovery of a solution to the announcement of the product. "And that's why I created" is still a great phrase here. Announce the product, give a few benefit-driven bullets, and then link to the sales page if they want to find out more about it. That's it.

Day 4—Pitch #2 (Core Benefit)

In day four's email, we are simply pitching the course. Lead with the core benefit of the course and how it will help the reader achieve a desired result or solve a specific problem. Include more details from the sales page, including a few powerful testimonials. Link to the sales page a few times so they can find out more.

I like to use the PS of this email to highlight the money-back guarantee so they can know their purchase is risk-free.

Day 5—Pitch #3 (Another Benefit)

And finally, we have one more straightforward pitch email (the third if you've been counting). All we want to do here is highlight another powerful benefit of the course, share more testimonials, and encourage the reader to check out the sales page for more information. Make a real plea here to the reader that this course will be great for them and that it's helped so many of your students.

Testimonials can and should dominate this email if you have enough. Other people's success with your course will always sell it better than anything you could say. Link to the sales page for information and include a PS that says to reply to you if they have any questions about the course.

WHY THIS EMAIL SEQUENCE WORKS

This five-day email sequence is such an effective way to sell your course because it's built on two things: **generosity and relevancy**. It's generous because it includes more free content, all of which is a surprise overdeliver. It's relevant because it builds off their interest in your lead magnet and then eventually offers a relevant course that can take your subscribers deeper and give them even greater results.

Another reason it works so well is because it gets to the pitch within the first few days of your prospect discovering you. I call this seven-day period of time beginning when they first discover your free content online as the *Golden Window of Sales*. Anecdotally, I have seen this be the best time to offer a product to someone. After the first week, interest wanes a bit more as life distracts them, and they forget about you.

Take advantage of the newness, of the excitement of them finding you, and bring them right to the virtual shelf where your awesome online course is on display. Also keep in mind that as you create and launch new products, you can extend this autoresponder sequence to add more valuable content emails and eventually lead to another pitch. And so on, and so on.

WHAT HAPPENS AFTER MY SUBSCRIBERS GO THROUGH THIS FUNNEL?

One question I get all the time when I teach about automated email funnels is, "What do I do with everyone on my email list after they've gone through my five-day sequence?" Well, the first thing you *don't* do is ignore them and move on. You want to cultivate your list and keep them engaged so that when you build and launch new products, they will be primed to listen to what you have to say.

With that in mind, there are two questions I want to answer for you right now: **How often should I email my list? And what should I email them about?**

So how often should you email your list? The answer is one word: regularly. For email to work, you need to create a regular rhythm that people will (subtly) count on. If you let weeks or months go by without an email, your audience will move on. Then, when you want to launch a new product or promote something, your emails will seem like they came out of nowhere, and they won't convert.

I used to email around three times a week. Just about every other day an email would go out from me. This keeps me in their inbox regularly without me needing to email every day. However, these days I'm down to one or two. I would recommend that you email your list once a week at minimum. No less.

And what should you be emailing these people? There are three things you should be sending:

- **Your latest content.** If you have a new blog post, video, or podcast episode, send it to your list. Don't assume they will ever come back to your website or channel to check it out. This is an easy way to stay top of mind and train them to expect valuable emails from you.
- **Something exclusive.** Occasionally send your email list something exclusive. This could be a bonus tip, article, thought, or testimony that might help or encourage them. I even will go so far as to *tell* them I'm not posting this anywhere else publicly, that they're only getting it because they are subscribed to my list.
- **Promotional emails.** This might sound obvious, but every now and then, you should be promoting something to your list. Whether a new product, or your main course, or a flash sale, be sure to sell to your list, at least quarterly. This is how you make money.

One final note on sending these mass-broadcast emails to your list: you'll want to be sure to exclude anyone who is still currently in your email funnel. They are already getting a daily email from you that's promoting your course, so you don't want to overwhelm them with two emails in a day that are unrelated to each other. A simple way to do this in a program like Kajabi is to create an automation that tags everyone who has already gone through your email sequence. That way when you send your weekly email out to the remainder of your list, you can send it only to people with that "completion" tag. Easy peasy.

EMAIL MARKETING STATS THAT MATTER

As you begin sending out emails each week and watching your automated email funnel doing its thing every day, there are a couple of stats you should be paying attention to inside your email marketing software back end.

The first is **open rate**. If nobody opens your emails, nothing else matters. Typical open rates for new lists are 40–50 percent and go down as your list grows to anywhere between 15 and 30 percent. I know it sounds crazy, but not everyone is going to open your emails. Even if they like you and your content, it just won't happen. People get a lot of email, don't check their inboxes every day, and sometimes just aren't interested in what you're emailing out that week. It doesn't mean they won't open the next one.

The second statistic to watch is **click-through rate**. If barely half of your subscribers will open your emails, an even smaller percentage of your list will actually click on any links you send them. My click-through rates usually range from 0.5 percent to 7 percent, depending on what I'm linking to. If it's a free piece of content, it will be higher. If it's a sales page for a product, it will be lower.

How to Increase Open and Click-Through Rates

You don't have to accept the email stats that you're getting. There are a few things you can do to get more people to open and click inside your emails.

- **Write better subject lines.** It's critical to think through your subject lines before you send an email. It's almost more important than the email itself. Describe what they want or create intrigue. Specific subject lines like "How to EQ Vocals" will work if it's relevant to what your audience wants. Also just creating curiosity with something like "Boom!" or "The day I wanted to quit" will work. You can also spice up subject lines with interesting and specific details. For example, you could turn "A great workout plan" into "The workout plan that helped me lose sixteen pounds in three weeks."
- **Have a more personal "from name."** In your email client, you can choose what your "from name" is. This is the name that shows up in your subscribers' inboxes. Many businesses put their brand names or company names here. I suggest you use your real name as the "from name" for the emails rather than

the name of your company. So, instead of emails coming from "Holistic Workouts," let's say, have them come from the owner, Jenny Smith. Or you can use a combination. My emails used to be from "The Recording Revolution," but then I switched them to "Graham (Recording Revolution)" so people would know it was from me.

- **Include more than one link.** The easiest way to increase your click-through rate is to simply give them more to click on. Assuming your email has a link in it that you want them to click, make sure you put that link in at least two places—not just at the bottom of the email.

- *Bold* **the links so they stand out.** This is such a simple thing, but bolding the text makes it pop in the mostly text-based email. Basic formatting in general can make an email more readable, and people are drawn to words in bold. So take advantage of that subtle suggestion and make the link text itself bold.

- **Don't write out the actual URL.** A lot of email clients will move your email to spam if it contains an actual http://www.MyAwesomeWebsite.com in it. To avoid that, I suggest you highlight some relevant text and make that a hyperlink to your desired URL.

- **And to that end, hyperlink the most critical phrase.** This is something many people miss. Whatever is blue/bolded/underlined will catch the reader's eye. So hyperlink what you want them to see. Go ahead and hyperlink the key sentence or phrase that speaks directly to their needs or desires. It can be entire paragraphs if need be.

- And let me finish by sharing the biggest tip of all when it comes to email: **be human!**

Don't write to a sea of people, and don't write like you're a company or organization. Write like you're a human trying to communicate with another human. Tell stories, share about your life, your opinions, and your experiences. When in doubt, ditch the marketing lingo and just be you. Doing so will allow you to connect with your audience much better.

And one more thing: always write for *one* person, not many people. Your audience will respond more to an email that seems like it's written to *them* and not to the masses.

YOUR ONLINE BUSINESS IS NOW EVERGREEN

Let's take a step back for a moment and just marvel at how far your online business has come. If you're at this step, you have validated your idea; created a presence online through regular, amazing, free content; built an email list of warm leads; designed your first online course and launched it to the world; and now you've automated the entire process. When you arrive at this point, your online business is officially evergreen. And this is where the fun truly starts.

In review, here are the six steps to building an automated knowledge-income stream:

1. Find your profitable idea.
2. Begin creating content to generate traffic.
3. Use your website to grow your email list.
4. Build your first online course.
5. Launch your course.
6. Automate your course in an email funnel.

In the next few chapters, I'm going to address some of the finer details and questions that come up for my students after they've launched or begun building their business. And we'll start with the role of social media and paid advertising in your online business.

Action Step:

Outline your five-day email funnel and brainstorm some powerful subject lines to go with them. Once you feel good about the direction of your emails, write them out, borrowing copy from your sales page as needed in the final three emails.

Chapter 9

SOCIAL MEDIA AND PAID ADS

The Right Way to Add Fuel to the Fire

Now that you know the formula for building a knowledge-income stream and getting paid to share what you know, I'd like to address just a couple more things to set you up for success as you take this journey into the joys of online business ownership. One of those things is a proper view of social media and its cousin, paid advertising.

You might have been wondering why I've spoken so little about social media in this book. And even though I've hopefully made the case that building your email list is more important than building a social media following, you might still have questions about how it fits into this business model. Allow me to address those questions in a moment. But first, I want to prove a point by sharing a mind-blowing stat with you.

As I write this, I am nearing the end of a twelve-month social media fast. That's right: for the past year, I have completely quit all social media—Twitter, Facebook, Instagram, all of it. I deleted those apps off my phone, I've logged out of them on my computer (and don't even remember my passwords), and I haven't interacted with a single person on any of those platforms.

But check this out. In that time span, my business has quintupled! I'm doing five times the revenue I was from a year ago. And in case you're wondering, no, I haven't run a single ad during that time either. All I've been doing for the past year is everything I just taught you. Creating content, growing my email list, and building digital products.

I say all this to reinforce what I've been teaching you this whole time—you don't need social media or paid ads to grow your business. Yet when people think about online businesses, they think social media. But as we've seen, the goal of your business isn't to build a big following—it's to build an email list of warm leads. So the question remains: What role *does* social media play in your business? Let's start by looking at three critical truths regarding social media.

SOCIAL MEDIA TRUTH #1—SOCIAL MEDIA WAS MADE TO BE A CONNECTING TOOL, NOT A SELLING TOOL

That distinction is critical to your using these platforms effectively. Even though you could jump on social media right now and pitch your course, membership, or coaching, it won't convert very well. Remember that study I referenced in chapter 5 about selling on email versus social media?

> *60 percent of consumers state that they have made a purchase as the result of a marketing message they received by email. On the flip side, only 12.5 percent of them even consider a buy button as a purchase driver on social media.* —*OptinMonster, 2019*

People don't go to these platforms in a buying mood. They go to be entertained, to stalk celebrities, or to be encouraged. They also follow people and brands they find interesting, inspirational, and valuable. That's where you fit in. You can easily show up on social and share nuggets of wisdom, inspiration, and encouragement around your topic or niche. This provides value and opens the door for further engagement and connection.

Social media platforms are great environments to poll your audience and get instant feedback. Use them to take the pulse on your audience to know what they want, need, or are frustrated with. This all helps you with your content strategy and product development. It will even help you write better sales copy.

SOCIAL MEDIA TRUTH #2—YOU DON'T HAVE TO BE EVERYWHERE AND POST EVERY DAY TO BE EFFECTIVE

One of the lies that's told over and over in marketing and business circles is that, in order to be successful, you must be present on every single social media platform, and on top of that, you must post every day and even multiple times a day. Lord help us.

Reality check: this line of thinking leads you down an endless black hole. There seem to be new social platforms emerging every week. Trends change, and the masses leave one platform for the next new thing all the time. It is impossible to exist everywhere, let alone do it well. In fact, the more consistent you are on one platform, the better you will be, rather than trying to spread yourself out over five platforms with a diluted effort.

And as it relates to posting all day every day, forget it. #Winning on social media isn't your goal. Connecting with your audience is. And actually, connecting with a specific purpose in mind. Which leads us to the third truth about social media.

SOCIAL MEDIA TRUTH #3—YOUR PRIMARY GOAL SHOULD BE TO STAY TOP OF MIND WITH YOUR AUDIENCE, ADD VALUE, AND POINT PEOPLE TO YOUR LEAD MAGNET

I want you to reread that third truth one more time.

This is the true purpose of any social media platform if you're running an online business. Not selling, not growing the biggest following, not getting the most likes or comments. Instead, your goal is to simply pop up in their world from time to time, remind them you exist and you have gobs of good stuff to share, and then invite them into a deeper relationship with you by offering them even more sweet goodness for free via your lead magnet.

This of course builds your email list, *which* you now know puts people into your automated email funnel that will pitch them a relevant online course and put money in your pocket. And that, my friend, is a beautiful thing.

With that perspective in mind, let's get granular and map out a manageable and effective social media strategy that you can implement in your online business.

YOUR SOCIAL MEDIA STRATEGY

- **Pick one or two platforms.** Decide which major platform (or two) where your ideal audience hangs out the most and commit to posting only there. This single decision will take most of the pressure off as you give yourself permission to only hang out in one or two places.
- **Use visuals.** We've become so visually driven that even Twitter (a primarily text-based platform) is filled with images and videos daily. And we've moved more heavily into video posting as the norm as well, thanks to SnapChat, Instagram Stories, and TikTok.
- **Offer free information.** Simply put: help people. Create posts that add value. Teach and share. Motivate. Highlight your weekly

content. Remember the value circle we discussed in chapter 2. Your social media posts represent the very beginning of that circle and must be drenched in value. That doesn't mean long posts, but it means posts that are worth your followers' time.

- **Ask questions and engage.** Social media is social. That means it shouldn't all be a monologue. Start and continue conversations with your followers. Ask their opinions. Ask for feedback. Poll them regularly. Get them engaged in what you're talking about and truly hang out with them virtually.

- **Build a tribe.** The goal isn't to grow as big of a generic following as you can. Your business only needs the right type of people to grow. So curate the type of followers who would be your ideal customers and make content for *them*.

- **Mention your lead magnet.** This is the best use of social media—regularly linking people to your amazing and free lead magnet as a resource so you can build your list. You don't have to do this with every post, but at least weekly have your call to action on social media be to download your lead magnet.

- **Find a sustainable strategy.** So much changes from month to month when it comes to what's "working" on social media, so focus on what *doesn't* change—the purpose behind using social media: connecting, engaging, and inviting people deeper into your ecosystem. If you follow what I've taught you so far in this book, an ecosystem is what you will have. And this system is designed to add massive value and generate money for you. If you have that already in place, then use social media to draw more people into it.

Now what about paid ads? What is the best way to leverage social media platforms like Facebook and Instagram to generate paid traffic for your business? Well, I think the first question you should be asking is: Should you even consider paid ads in the first place?

DON'T PAY FOR ADS IF . . .

Even though I'm not a fan of running paid ads and I don't use them personally in my business, I'm OK with you doing it. However, I'm of the opinion that you shouldn't consider spending a dime on ads if any of these three things are true.

- **You haven't exhausted all free resources.** Are you faithfully working your content-marketing strategy? Do you consistently publish great content at least weekly? Are you collaborating with other content creators and guest posting? Have you leveraged social media, and are you serving your audience there for free? If not, then why spend money when you have free strategies at your disposal?
- **You haven't started selling products.** As you know by now, the reality is you don't need paid ads to find people to sell your products to. That's what your free content will do for you. So my suggestion would be to make some money first, and *then* consider ads.
- **You don't have your system in place.** Too many people throw money at paid advertising hoping and believing that it will lead to guaranteed results. The problem is that paid ads really are only as effective as your system. Have you proven and perfected your online business ecosystem yet? Ideally, you should have lots of happy customers, testimonials, and a stress-tested system in place before considering ads.

Honestly, most businesses shouldn't use or need paid ads to get customers, make good money, or even scale. Because of simple content marketing and strategic partnerships here and there, I have built two million-dollar-per-year businesses, and I haven't had to spend a dime on advertising.

That being said, if you've decided that you *are* going to run paid ads, the most effective way to reach customers is through targeted Facebook ads.

WHY FACEBOOK IS SO POWERFUL

- **It's where the people are.** As of 2021, Facebook has roughly 2.8 billion active users. With only 4.6 billion people with active internet access worldwide, that's 60 percent of the world's internet users on the platform.
- **You can target your ideal customer.** Facebook's powerful targeting features make it ideal to zero in on *only* the people most likely to dig your stuff. You can choose to advertise only to people who like or follow your competitors, or who purchase certain products that are relevant to your niche. You can even upload your email list to Facebook and have it look at those people on your list who are Facebook users and find other people on the platform who like similar things.
- **You only pay when it works.** This is something called pay-per-click advertising, and it's amazing. Instead of paying to air a TV commercial regardless of whether it gets customers or not, with Facebook ads, you can only pay when your ad does its job. You simply set a max daily budget and only pay for an ad when someone clicks on it. Brilliant.

That all being said, here's the key to making Facebook ads work: you must track, track, track. What do I mean by that? What you *don't* want to do is just throw money at Facebook ads and see if sales seem to go up. That kind of sloppiness will cost you a fortune. Instead, you want to use something called the Facebook Pixel. This is a custom piece of code that Facebook will give you to paste on your landing page or sales page. You then can track it to see exactly how much revenue a hundred dollars' worth of ads brings in.

Facebook Ad Example

Let's do some math and walk through a simple example of how I might run a Facebook ad and know whether or not it's working.

Let's say you spent $200 on Facebook ads last week. Because of the Pixel (remember that piece of code on your opt-in thank-you page), you can see you got four hundred clicks and made five sales. Some quick math tells me that this ad is costing you forty dollars a sale. Is that good or bad? Well, it depends. If your product sells for fifty dollars, that means you're making a profit on the ads, and you can pump more money into them. In that scenario, your ad spend is justified because you spent $200 but made $250 worth of sales from it.

If, on the other hand, your product sold for less, then you could easily see that you might actually be losing money on the ads, even with some sales coming through. Either way, you know where you stand. The question is: What do you do to improve the ad conversion?

That's another great thing about Facebook ads; you can create multiple versions of the same ad and split test them to see which performs better, and for what reason. Basic changes like tweaking the headline or the image can make a huge difference. Make a few slightly different versions and see if you get more sales for the same investment. You can of course also change what audience you show that ad to, testing out what ad performs better for whom.

Finally, keep this in mind: **even if you break even on ads, it can be worth it**. How can that be? Quite simply because you are essentially gaining new customers for free who will likely buy more of your products later. Again, it's not the same as actually making a profit today; if done as part of your lead-generating strategy, it could mean potential profit down the line.

KNOW WHAT REALLY DRIVES YOUR BUSINESS

At the end of the day, I want you to remember one thing: posting to social media and running ads are tools. They aren't the engine of your business, but they might be helpful in making your business run a little faster. That's up to you to decide.

And speaking of engines, if you boil down online business into its essence, there are actually only four core things you need to be doing week in and week out in your business to drive what I call the *Income Engine*, and that's what I want to share with you in the next chapter.

Action Step:

Decide what one or two social media platforms you will commit to showing up on and make a plan on how often you will post and engage with your audience there. Also, go back through this chapter and decide if it makes sense for you to run paid ads in your business right now (or ever).

Chapter 10

THE INCOME ENGINE

The Four Core Things That Will Drive Your Business

There are two distinct stages of a successful business—the start-up phase and the growth phase. What we've covered up until this point has all had to do with the start-up phase. If you've gotten to this point, you have achieved a lot. Let's quickly review what you've done so far.

At this stage in your business:

- You **have a website** that is optimized.
- You're creating **regular and valuable content**.
- You're **growing your email list** every month.
- You've **launched your product** to your list.
- Your autoresponder is set up to **bring in revenue automatically**.

Pat yourself on the back, my friend, because what you've accomplished is remarkable. Most people can only dream about having an online business that puts money in their pockets day and night, whether they're working or not. But I have a warning for you.

Now is not the time to sit back, sip a cold beverage, and wait for the money to roll in. You're so close to a beautiful, growing, automatic-income business. But you need one final thing: a system and plan to follow from here on out. This is so crucial to your long-term success, but unfortunately, this is where most passive-income evangelists leave you hanging.

THE PASSIVE-INCOME DREAM

Most education and training on this subject only gets you this far. Once you've launched your online course or built your evergreen email funnel, these gurus pretty much assume you're set and leave you believing it's all gravy from here on out. In fact, this is what their core message tends to be to online business owners who are wrapping up this start-up phase.

- "Once you get it all set up, you won't have to touch it again!"
- "Take a year off, live at the beach, and watch all the money flow into your bank account!"
- "If you ever need to crank it up, just buy some Facebook ads!"

This isn't magic. It's a business—and business takes work, especially if you want to move from the start-up phase to the growth phase of business. Think of these two phases as flying an airplane. The start-up phase has to do with building the airplane, piece by piece. Then putting it on a runway, fueling the engines, and getting up to a speed fast enough for the wings to catch lift.

But once the plane is in the air, the pilot shouldn't just jump out and parachute down to the beach. There is still work to be done to maintain altitude and keep the plane in flight, albeit less work than building the plane and taking off. **The growth phase of your business is a lot like that—it still takes work, but less work than you think.** There are only four things you need to be doing.

These four components make up what I call the Income Engine. Consider the Income Engine your four-part plan for what to do week in and week out in your business. No more guessing. No more wondering if you should try this tactic or that. Just four simple things that will drive your business forward and grow your income over time.

COMPONENT #1—CREATE REGULAR CONTENT

I hate to break it to you (and I want to be as clear as I can here), but you should never stop making content. Period. Full stop. Content is the life-blood of your online business. It's the fuel for the engine, and without that fuel, the engine will eventually die. If you could only do *one* thing each week for your business, it should be to create content.

This is something many smart online business owners miss. They've worked hard to build a brand, create a ton of amazing content, build their list, and launch their product. Once they see sales coming in, they imme-diately think their content days are behind them. With dollar signs in their eyes, they are drawn to more "advanced" things like marketing tactics, bet-ter sales copy, and running ads. They end up posting less often, and their organic traffic begins to dry up, ironically forcing them to rely completely on paid ads. And now they've created an ad monster that gobbles up their profit and raises their stress levels.

I teach my students to make regular new content the priority. **Make a sacred vow with yourself that never will a week go by without you uploading something new to YouTube, your podcast, or blog.** Publish something new even when you don't feel like it, even when you feel like you've run out of ideas. Because here's the truth: if you pay attention to your audience, you will *never* run out of ideas. Take that from someone who has been publishing content every week for twelve years straight.

Listen to your audience's needs, wants, and interests to help determine what content to publish next. Read comments, emails, and social media DMs to see what follow-up questions arise from your latest content. Keep all of these questions and suggestions in a Google Doc and reference it when you get stumped.

Also, remember that every day you have new visitors. These are new people who have just discovered your material for the first time. Don't assume everyone consuming your content has seen all your other content.

It is absolutely OK to revisit previous topics or questions over and over again. Each time you revisit previous material in a new piece of content, you will be reinforcing your philosophy and methods, which will be a good reminder for your veteran followers and will provide great *new* insights for your latest subscribers. Also, each time you teach on a familiar topic, it will inherently be slightly different as you aren't a static robot. You are a living thing that grows and changes over time. Thus, your latest take on a subject will bring with it subtle, fresh nuances.

I'll say it again: nothing matters more than new content. And just a little bonus tip: you don't have to *make* the content weekly. You can batch record, write, or create content weeks and months in advance if you wish. This will allow you to take time off work to travel and rest, all while new content is scheduled to go out into the world—automatically!

COMPONENT #2—GROW YOUR EMAIL LIST

A close second to content creation (and irrevocably tied to it) is growing your email list. If the whole point of content is discoverability and credibility, then getting people on your list is critical because that's what allows you to offer them your evergreen online course, which is how you get paid. But a key point I'd like to make is this: **the size of your list doesn't matter as much as whether new people are joining it**.

There's something called lead decay, and it relates to the value of an email subscriber. Basically, over the years, I've seen that newer subscribers, people on my list who have been subscribed for fewer than thirty days, tend to buy more readily than older subscribers, people who have been on my list for over three months or so. This likely has to do with two things. One, newer subscribers are excited for what you have to offer now. How do we know that? Because they just found you and just downloaded your lead magnet. Second, older subscribers might have stopped noticing and opening your emails, which can create a cycle of them not noticing or opening your future emails as well. Hence, they might not see what you offer as much as someone who is newer.

The solution to this lead decay is simple: get new people on your list. Beyond getting more eyeballs through your weekly content uploads, here are three ways to grow your email list:

- **Create new lead magnets.** So far, you've created one core lead magnet that should appeal to just about anyone who consumes your free content. One way to increase email opt-in conversions (i.e., get more people to subscribe) is to create more niche lead magnets that are focused and more relevant to the specific topics you cover in your content.

   For example, I have a Radio-Ready Guide lead magnet for Recording Revolution that gives you a step-by-step plan to make better-sounding recordings. But when I do videos on a tool called compression, I make sure to mention my seven-step compression checklist guide as a more relevant lead magnet. This converts even better to people who are already learning about compression. Make sense?

- **Partner with other content creators.** There's nothing saying you have to grow your email list from your audience only. Why not siphon a few hundred (or thousand) emails from someone *else's* audience as well? In all seriousness, it's a legit strategy that can be a win-win for everyone involved.

   This all goes back to guest posting or content swapping with someone who has a similar audience. They could be in your niche or, even better, a complementary niche. Make friends, network, see if you can add value to someone else's brand and audience in exchange for being able to offer one of your lead magnets.

- **Use social media to drive opt-ins.** Remember that everything you do on social media should point people back to a relevant lead-magnet opt-in on your site. As important as it is to engage and build your audience on these platforms, don't get so caught up in trying to go viral that you miss the chance to usher your followers over to your email list and "lock in those gains" before the algorithms change again.

Remember just how important your email list is to your online business, both now and in the future. Having an audience is key, but being able to reach out to them directly whenever you want and without a middleman is critical to you being able to make sales and live the life you've dreamed of. As you create regular content, stay dedicated to getting as many targeted leads onto your email list as you can, and you'll be in business for a long time.

COMPONENT #3—NURTURE YOUR LIST

Staying on the topic of email lists, let's talk about what to do with yours. Remember the whole lead-decay thing I shared a moment ago? Well, let's talk about some ways to slow down or reverse that decay altogether.

Like I said, the size of your list doesn't matter nearly as much as the quality of your list. Having a list of a hundred thousand people where only 5 percent of them ever engage with your content is actually worse than having a list of only ten thousand where 60 percent open and consume your material. Engagement is the metric we online business owners really should care about, not sheer numbers.

I have over three hundred thousand on one email list and only ten thousand on the other. And while my ego gets a boost from the bigger list, it's the smaller list that has more engagement right now and leads to more sales. I'm not saying more people on your list isn't the goal (we just said it was in the last component of the Income Engine); I am saying that the quality of that list is just as important. Here are a few ways to help nurture your list to keep the quality of your subscribers (and therefore the potential engagement) high.

- **Treat them like VIPs.** Your email subscribers should mean more to you than your YouTube viewers or subscribers. They should mean more to you than your podcast listeners or the people who leave comments on your blog. Those are all wonderful people, but if they haven't given you their email address, they aren't as high on the totem pole. But inevitably, most online business owners spend most of their time catering to the casual follower on social media rather than their own email subscribers, which is a big mistake.

I recommend you treat your email subscribers like VIPs. And you can do this very easily: simply send exclusive content to them regularly. And by exclusive, I mean content you don't post publicly. This could be a quick video you shoot on your phone, bringing them behind the scenes into your world. This could be a bonus PDF guide you put together that they would find valuable. Or you could even do a private live Q&A call to coach them and answer their questions.

All this does is increase the odds of them opening up future emails from you and engaging with your promotions because they will have been trained to assume that you only send valuable stuff and your emails are worth paying attention to.

- **Ask their opinion.** Another easy way to increase engagement and make them feel valuable is to treat them like a real friend whose opinion you care about. By that, I mean, quite simply: Ask them questions. Solicit their opinions and feedback on a given subject or topic. Show them that you value their thoughts and insights.

    You can do this with a formal survey, or you can simply ask them to reply back to your email with their answers. And here's the kicker: if they reply to you, be sure to respond to their answers. This shows them that you're a real person on the other end and that you value them enough to pay attention to what they say. This does wonders for their loyalty and engagement with your brand.

    Bonus tip: if you want to get more responses to your survey, consider incentivizing the process by offering a free course, coaching call, or some other gift in a random drawing of survey submissions.

And one final thought here on email-list nurturing. The point is to simply add value to your subscribers so they stay subscribed and engaged with your content. **That doesn't mean *you* have to be the one adding value. You can simply be the curator of someone *else's* great ideas or insights.**

If you read a good article that makes a great point, share it with your list. If you stumble across a helpful YouTube channel that fills in a gap from your teaching, share it. Your list will be grateful to you for sending it their way. It matters little if you created that content yourself.

COMPONENT #4—BUILD NEW PRODUCTS

I'd like to point out that the first three components of the Income Engine all help you sell more of your *current* online course. By doing those three things, you will increase your income substantially, without the need for adding any new products to your lineup. And that is truly remarkable. You see, so many people move on to building new products too quickly without ever giving their *first* product a fair shot at making money.

As I pointed out earlier, I've made over $1 million on a little $99 course I launched over a decade ago, all because of these first three components of the Income Engine. That's amazing! That being said, to truly scale, you *will* need to build and sell more than one product in your business. So how many products should you have? And how often should you release a new one? Here's a simple framework I suggest you follow, especially if you're running this business on the side: **commit to launching something new every year that you can sell**.

That's it. No need to launch multiple courses a year, or rush to build your first membership. Instead, make it a goal to launch one new thing a year and go from there. In five years, you'll likely have a fully developed product suite. And, hey, if you have the time and margin to launch more often than that, go for it. I launched on average two to three new products a year for my first three years. But I was working full-time on my business, so I had the bandwidth.

"What else can I sell?"

You might already be asking the question, so I'll just get down to it. When it comes to launching new products for your online business, there are some tried-and-true options that work well. I've built and sold *all* of these, and I can vouch for them as part of a strategic product suite. That being said, feel free to pick and choose which of these most interests you as you begin scaling your business. There is no *right* order to launch them in.

- **Build a more niche second course.** If you already launched a flagship online course that covers your audience's biggest needs, it can be a great idea to zoom in. You can create a more niched product or course in a specific area. This might even be a smaller mini course (two to three hours of content), but it gets more granular in details on that subject.
- **Offer an ultrapremium product.** Instead of going mini, you can go big and create a high-ticket product at ten to one hundred times the cost of your core course. My first premium course was a $600 course on freelancing as an audio engineer. It was a stretch for my audience who was used to buying $100 courses from me, but for the right person, it was worth it as it helped them create an income from their audio skills.
- **Create a membership/community.** A natural complement to your online courses is a paid membership that gives your students a powerful community and access to you. Memberships are great back-end products to a course because your students will have follow-up questions and want to go deeper. Plus, they'll want accountability from a community of like-minded people. Remember, a good membership includes the three Cs: content, coaching, and community.
- **Promote affiliate products.** You don't even have to launch new products of your own. You can simply partner with someone else to promote *their* product to your list and make a tidy profit. I've promoted other people's courses as well as software products like Kajabi. Both have paid handsomely.
- **Create a group coaching product or mastermind.** One way to scale is not wide (more customers) but deep (high price and more access to you). You can do this by selling a high-priced, multiweek or -month course that is conducted live with ten to

twelve students. The intimate size and close proximity to you can allow you to command high prices per month and can be a lot of fun as you get to work with some of your best students.

- **Host a live event.** In a world of online training, the ultimate luxury is learning in person. You could create a live workshop or retreat with some of your top customers, charge high-end prices, and give your students not only education but also an experience they will never forget. I've hosted multiple two- and three-day in-person workshops and had students from all over the country attend. They are always a blast! The key is to manage costs and charge enough to make a profit.

There you have it. The next five-plus years of your business mapped out. **Launch one new product a year and keep feeding the other three components of your Income Engine, and your revenue will only grow and grow.** Any combination of these product ideas can work marvelously. Some of my friends started with a mastermind. Others started with live events. Most start with a course and build from there. Whatever feels right to you, do it. All that matters is that you create new things to offer your people over time.

In review, once your business is launched, all you need to focus on week in and week out are these four things:

1. **Publishing fresh content**
2. **Growing your email list**
3. **Nurturing your email list**
4. **Building new products**

Visually you can think of the Income Engine as another circle that, once you get it spinning, will continue to spin faster and faster, generating more and more income for you.

I know what you might be thinking: *It almost seems too simple.* I can tell you that from teaching thousands of people how to build and scale their online businesses, most people think there has to be more to it than

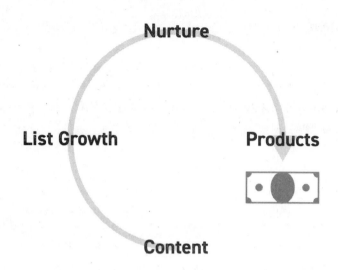

this. Perhaps some new marketing trick or having a video go viral on You-Tube or TikTok. But there isn't.

Recently, one of my students, Jacques, who is a member of my Epic Mastermind (and a seven-figure earner in his own right), asked me about my business model. He drew up a diagram (virtually identical to the one above) that he felt represented how my business worked from what he could tell from the outside and what I've shared in the group. He sent it to me and everyone in the mastermind and said, "What am I missing about your business model here. It can't be this simple, can it?" The answer of course is yes—it *is* that simple.

Remember: just because it's simple doesn't mean it doesn't work.

This simple model will get your business into the multiple six figures each year, easily. From there, you can of course begin building a small team of part-time contractors to help free up your time and give you more flexibility, but it's not necessary. Just follow the four components of the Income Engine, and you'll be set.

We've covered a lot of ground here, but as with most things you read about, it's only head knowledge until you apply it. In our final chapter, I want to give you some parting thoughts on how and why you need to simply get started. Without taking that first step, your life will never change.

Action Step:

Take the four components of the Income Engine and map them out into weekly, monthly, and yearly tasks. How often will you post content? When will you launch your next product? Put dates on a calendar if that helps you.

Chapter 11

WHY SIMPLY STARTING IS ALL THAT MATTERS

Back in 2020, the world was waking up to the reality of a global pandemic. Jobs were lost, industries were shuttered, and people began looking for ways to create an income online. While a hard year for many, this turned out to be a great year for someone like me who teaches normal people how to build online businesses.

What was most interesting was all of the people (including close friends) who reached out to me to say virtually the same thing: "*Graham, I see now how important it is to have an income stream that is created online. I'm ready now. I just wish I would have started this whole thing a few years ago.*"

And I feel their pain. The moment you *need* the money, it feels too late to get started. For so many whose jobs or businesses were lost due to COVID-19 and the lockdowns, there was immediate pressure to make money right away. Unfortunately, that's not how this works. **But just because it would have been nice to have started their online businesses a few years back doesn't mean they shouldn't start today!**

There's a popular Chinese proverb that goes something like this: "The best time to plant a tree was twenty years ago. The second-best time is now." The point couldn't be clearer: Don't wait. Start now! But most people won't start. And there's a big reason why: fear.

FEAR IS A LIAR

Most people are afraid to start something new. They worry that their idea won't be good enough to work, and so they wait until either they feel 100 percent ready or they feel sure they can execute it perfectly. My concern is that after reading this entire book, you might feel so overwhelmed that you don't start. I get it.

We've covered a lot up till now, but you don't have to do it all at once. When it comes to creating a knowledge-income stream, what matters most is simply starting. Don't wait another day to plant your seeds in the ground. Start now and grow as you go.

Author and speaker Jon Acuff has a great (and aptly titled) book called *Start*, and in it, he makes the case that starting is really the only part of life you can control, and it's usually fear that keeps you from doing it.

> *[Fear] is schizophrenic. Fear tends to argue both sides of the coin, leaving you absolutely no room to stand. Here are two of the complete opposite things it will tell you: "Don't chase your dream at all." And, "If you chase your dream, you have to do it all at once."*

He goes on to say: "The starting line is the only line you completely control. The start is the only moment you're the boss of. The finish? Don't kid yourself. That's months, if not years away."

Read those last two quotes again. Acuff is acknowledging two powerful truths that can set you free and lead you to success beyond your wildest dreams if you internalize them:

1. **Fear will tell you to either give up before you start or pressure you into having to do it all at once. Those are not the only two choices.**

2. **The only thing you can control is the starting line. The results are completely out of your hands, so don't worry about them.**

Can I let you in on a little secret? I'm writing this chapter not from theory but from personal experience. And not just experience long ago, but as recent as yesterday. Believe it or not, fear is something I still struggle with today.

BE AFRAID (AND THEN PUNCH FEAR IN THE FACE)

Fear is a reality. We can't escape it. The key is to stop, acknowledge the fear, and then (like Jon Acuff's subtitle says) "punch fear in the face" and move forward with your life. While I'm not a pro at this, I do have a lot of experience with it.

If you remember from chapter 1 of this book, I had no idea what I was doing when I started my first knowledge-income stream, the Recording Revolution, in 2009. But I started. I didn't even know what an online course or lead magnet was. I could never have predicted it would grow into what it has become (a seven-figure business that reaches millions of people a year) and open up so many doors for me. Doors that included starting my personal brand, turning that into another seven-figure business, and writing this book!

Not only did I have no idea what I was doing along the way, but also I've been afraid the entire time. Here are just a few of the fears I've had during my career:

- afraid of it not working
- afraid that I'll embarrass myself or say something stupid
- afraid of what my family thought of me blogging every week and not getting a "real job"
- afraid that people will think I'm greedy for wanting a second business

- afraid that I don't belong in the business-coaching space and that I should have stayed in the music space

And yet, I started anyway. And that has made all the difference. But if you think there's more to success than that, you'd be right. There's a part two to this. If simply starting is the most important step you can take, then the second would have to be not quitting. These things take time. All valuable endeavors do.

SLOW GROWTH ALWAYS WINS

I once heard billionaire investor and entrepreneur Chamath Palihapitiya (an early senior executive at Facebook) say in an interview: "The faster you build it, that is the half-life. It will get destroyed in the same amount of time." He went on to say that he much prefers slow compounding companies like Amazon. They aren't splashy, but they grow year after year because they are consistent. Your business should be the same.

Don't rush to build your business for quick money. Slow growth always wins. Why? Because it's stable. The slow, methodical, brick-by-brick approach to growing your online business gives you time to learn and adapt, strengthening you for a long and prosperous life in business. If you grow too fast, you might not be around long enough to enjoy it. When I started my first online business in the music space, there were ten or so other really successful brands doing the exact same thing. They were interested in growing quickly. Twelve years later, of those ten, only three are still around that I know of.

Give yourself permission to grow slowly. As cliché as it sounds, this isn't a sprint; it's a marathon. And with that in mind, allow me to give you some final suggestions as we close our time together.

Some Suggestions for Starting

- **Don't quit your day job until you have enough cash to sustain you for six months to a year, or until your business is covering at least half of your bills.** It was a stressful time for me to have to build my first business without any real income, and I wouldn't wish that on you at all. Keeping one income stream while you begin building your knowledge-income stream will serve as a bridge and help you stay in the game long enough to get traction.

- **Find three to six hours a week in your schedule to commit to building your knowledge-income stream.** That's thirty minutes a day at minimum. You can do it a little at a time or chunk it all on the weekends. Some of my students wake up an hour earlier to work on their business before the family wakes up and their day begins. Some stay up later and do the same. Whatever fits you and your family's rhythms, just block it off and make it sacred time.

- **Only plan out the next twelve months. Anything longer than that and you'll get ahead of yourself.** Spend the first six months researching and beginning to create content consistently. Spend the next six months building and launching your first course. If you can go faster, that's fine, but remember that you want to build a strong foundation for your business so you can grow a moneymaking machine for years to come. Nothing great was ever built quickly.

ALREADY STARTED BUT FEELING STUCK?

Perhaps you picked up this book in hopes not of *starting* your online business but of *restarting* it. Or maybe you've been chipping away at this thing for a year or two with little to nothing to show for it. Whatever the reason for your plateau, don't be hard on yourself. It happens to everyone at some point. Here are some common places my students get stuck in their online business journeys and some of my best advice I offer for getting traction again.

"I'm posting content each week but not seeing any more traffic/ views."

The first thing to remember with content marketing (which we covered in chapter 4) is that it takes time. It's a long game. If you've been faithfully publishing blog posts, YouTube videos, or podcasts weekly for six months or so, the truth is you're still in the early phases.

It takes months, sometimes years, for Google and YouTube to find your content and begin "serving it up" in search results for your future audience to find. Don't quit.

One of my students, Brad, is a financial coach who had been faithfully uploading YouTube videos for almost two years with low view counts. And then one day, one of his videos "popped" and was picked up by YouTube. He went from getting one hundred to two hundred views on a video to over one hundred thousand in twenty-four hours! He couldn't believe it.

But that's how content works. Eventually, something will catch fire, which will lead to more traffic on your other content. Most of your uploads will be average, and that's OK. You only need one, two, or three pieces of content to blow up in order to see exponential audience growth.

The lesson? Keep posting. Keep paying attention to what your current audience likes. Adjust accordingly and don't give up.

"I launched my course, but no one (or hardly anyone) bought it."

This hurts. I've been there. It never feels good to work hard on outlining, filming, editing, uploading, and marketing a product only to have it not sell well, or not sell at all. Don't get too discouraged, though, because there are two things to consider here.

First, remember the rule of thumb: when you launch your products to your email list, you should expect only 0.5 to 1 percent of them to buy. If you have a list of one hundred people and you don't make a single sale, it almost makes sense. Statistically, only one-half of one person would buy (on the low end). So make sure it's not an audience-size problem first.

Second, if your audience size isn't the issue, then the offer just wasn't the right fit for your people. Or, more likely, it wasn't positioned well. Meaning, they don't *think* it's a good fit for them—even if it might be.

This comes back to the sales-copy process we discussed in chapter 7. Your course might be perfect for them, and it might be the right price, but if you haven't conveyed the true benefits to your people, then they won't buy. Take some time to review the three-step sales-copy formula I showed you and make sure you've addressed each of those elements clearly in your sales page.

And when in doubt, ask your people why they didn't purchase. A simple email humbly asking why they didn't decide to join will give you some real data points as to what the disconnect might be. Adjust your sales copy, emails, and launch strategy accordingly next time.

"I can never seem to finish anything (my course, sales copy, email sequence) and get this business off the ground."

I get it: life is full and busy. You may feel like you've been squeezing every extra hour out of your day trying to launch this thing but there just isn't enough time in the day. If you'll allow me to be blunt, the more likely reason you haven't finished what you're working on is that you are just procrastinating.

Chances are good that there's some combination of perfectionism and insecurity (i.e., fear) that's keeping you from hitting "send" on that launch campaign or "publish" on that sales page.

The reality is you'll never have a perfect sales page. You'll never have a perfect email funnel. You'll never have a perfect online course. Someone will hate it. Yourself included. But none of that matters. All you need is "good enough," and you can become a millionaire. I'm living proof!

The key to online business (or any business, for that matter) is to get it good enough and just put it out there. Yes, it's scary. Yes, you might have typos. Yes, it could likely be better. But one thing is certain: if you don't put your stuff out there, no one will buy. I'd much rather you launch it now and improve it later. Once you make that first sale, you'll get some wind in your sails that will carry you through to the next week, month, and year of your business. That momentum is powerful and needed in order to sustain a successful online business.

So don't let fear or the illusion of perfect hold you back from finishing whatever it is you're working on in your business right now. Get it good enough and put it out there.

There you go. You now have everything you need to go out and build a profitable side or full-time online business by monetizing your knowledge, skills, and passions—all from the comfort of your home.

WHAT WOULD A KNOWLEDGE-INCOME STREAM DO FOR YOU?

As you begin taking steps on this amazing online business journey, I want you to get clear on why you're doing this in the first place. Way back at the beginning of this book, I asked you these two questions:

If you had an extra $1,000 a month or $5,000 a month coming in from your own knowledge-income stream, what would that mean in your life? **If your online business only took twenty hours a week to run and generated a full-time income, how would your life improve?**

Here's a short list of some possible answers to those questions. You could do any of these—or all of them:

- pay off your student loans or car debt
- take a three-day weekend every weekend
- max out your retirement account
- work only half days, cutting out at lunch every day
- save up a down payment for a house (or pay off your house early)
- take your kids to school each morning and pick them up in the afternoon
- put your kids through private school
- have time to exercise every day and get more than eight hours of sleep
- spend more time volunteering at your church

What is *your* vision of life with a fully online, automated business in place that pays your bills and frees up your time? Get clear on that, as it will keep you motivated as you start down this path.

AN ENDLESS RESOURCE FOR YOU

Finally, this is not where the conversation or the relationship has to end. While a book is a static resource, my website is a living, breathing training ground for up-and-coming digital entrepreneurs like yourself. If you ever get stuck or need motivation, be sure to listen to my weekly podcast, *The Graham Cochrane Show*, on Apple Podcasts or YouTube. Or just navigate to GrahamCochrane.com, and it's all there as well.

My hope is that I can be your ongoing virtual business coach, teaching you and cheering you on as you build your audience and serve them well. Remember: you have something valuable to share, and the world needs to hear it. You don't need to be like anyone else or present in any specific way. You simply need to take what you know and your unique perspective on things and give it away.

I will leave you with two Bible verses that I believe summarize not only this business model but also the way life truly works:

King Solomon wrote, "*One gives freely, yet grows all the richer; another withholds what he should give, and only suffers want. Whoever brings blessing will be enriched, and one who waters will himself be watered*" (Proverbs 11:24–25 ESV).

And the apostle Paul echoed those thoughts when he said, "*Whoever sows sparingly will also reap sparingly, and whoever sows bountifully will also reap bountifully*" (2 Corinthians 9:6).

My hope for you is that you take what you've learned here and you sow a lot of good seeds in the world and serve a lot of people. Because at the end of the day, that's all we're doing in business: serving. And what is serving? Giving of ourselves for the benefit of someone else.

And, honestly, I can't think of a more beautiful and worthy pursuit in life than that!

ACKNOWLEDGMENTS

This book would not exist without the help (both directly and indirectly) of some amazing people who I'd like to thank publicly here.

To Shay, my wife and best friend, thank you for supporting me through our entire marriage, both during the good times and the bad times. You were there at the beginning when I was freaking out that I had no job and no prospects of making money. You believed in me and gave me the freedom to sit in that little home office and begin to discover this thing called online business. Thank you for your patience, faith, and support. It has meant the world to me.

To my beautiful daughters, Chloe and Vera, you grew up with my business so you never saw Daddy sitting in a cubicle at a job he hated. For that I am grateful. I pray you never stop using your talents, gifts, and creativity. They are the key to unlocking your God-given purpose in life and work!

To my Mom and Dad, thank you for giving me a loving and supportive home to grow up in. Thank you also for supporting my education, not only academically but in the arts as well. For letting me play music, act on stages, play with recording equipment, and go to concerts. You both gave me so many opportunities to succeed and I am forever grateful.

To my one and only brother, Wes, thank you for being my biggest cheer-leader and lifelong friend. Thank you for always being interested in and excited with my work. You make me feel important and cool!

To my Grandpa Ken, thank you for giving your resources so generously to me and my brother so we could go to camps, do sports, and even go to college debt free. Turns out I became an author like you! I wish you could see me now.

To my Grandma Terry, thanks for watching my YouTube videos and send-ing me a handwritten note from across the country telling me what you liked about them. You've always supported me no matter what I've been into.

To my one and only uncle, Steve, thank you for teaching me the impor-tance of reading to my kids at a young age. It's helped them become avid readers, which increases the likelihood of them reading *this* book.

To my in-laws, Bill and Joanne, thank you for trusting me to provide for your daughter. Especially when I lost my job and twelve years later have still not found another one.

To my grandmother-in-law Pat, thank you for being excited that I'm now a published author. I'm finally doing something that you can wrap your head around, and for that I'm grateful!

To my friend Jordan Raynor, thank you for taking the time to help me write my proposal and find an agent. Your coaching and mentorship through this entire process has been invaluable. Thank you for giving me actionable homework and critiques early in the process. This book would literally not exist if it weren't for you.

To my friend and business partner Daiyaan Ghani, thank you for teaching me so much about online business. Not only did you help me take the Recording Revolution to the next level, you opened my eyes to so many subtle nuances of business and marketing that have enabled me to help so many people in my new endeavors. Much of this book was inspired by what we've done together and what I've picked up from you along the way.

To Joe Gilder, thank you for being such a friend in the online space since before I ever launched. You were the first "competitor" ever to promote my stuff to your audience, and for that I am forever grateful. So glad we were able to create some amazing products together and serve a bunch of people.

To Ashlee Proffitt, thank you for reviewing early versions of this book's cover and helping me and my designer land on the final one.

To my editor, Katie Dickman, thank you for reading this book more times than I have and making me sound like a smart author. Also, thanks for not crushing my spirit when you had suggestions or revisions!

To Brigid Pearson, thank you for designing such an awesome cover for this book. I love how it feels approachable, creative, and not like a typical stuffy business book.

To Mallory Hyde, thank you for helping me get the word out for this book. Your honesty and transparency about the marketing process has been so welcome and I know that the success of this book has largely been due to your work.

To Matt Holt, thank you for taking a chance on me as a first-time author. You understood the vision of me wanting to publish books in the physical world while still building video content in the digital world and so your partnership means a lot. I'm proud of what we've done together!

To Steve Piersanti at Berrett-Koehler, thank you for those initial Zoom calls where you helped me shape the proposal and positioning of this book in its infancy. Thank you also for the book title research you helped me conduct. We ended up going with your suggestions! Even though we didn't end up working together, I am forever grateful for your kind words, wisdom, and experience. I knew right away that you believed in me and this book and that meant a lot.

To my agent, DJ Snell, thank you for being excited about this book and taking me on as a client. Your guidance and suggestions during the entire proposal shopping process were critical to me finding the right publisher to work with. I literally would not have a book deal if it weren't for your help.

To Ramit Sethi, thanks for being an inspiration for both of my businesses. I've learned so much from you over the years, but one of the most important memories I have is that one phone call where I asked you about starting my second business. You gave me so much clarity and "permission" to launch my personal brand, and for that I am grateful.

To Tim Ferriss, thank you for teaching me the power of valuing not just money but time and flexibility. It has had a profound impact on my businesses and teachings.

To Jon Acuff, thank you for inspiring me to "start" something new even after I already had grown successful and comfortable in my first business. I keep coming back to your book.

To all my Recording Revolution students, thank you for supporting me over the years. Without you watching my videos and buying my products, this book wouldn't exist because my business wouldn't exist.

And to all my current Graham Cochrane students, thank you for inspiring me to continue to teach others this business model. Your stories of success fuel me to keep preaching the message and helping more people transition into work they love and living and giving more.

And most importantly, thank you, Jesus, for giving me life, purpose, and a future. All I have is a gift from you and so I am doing my best to steward it well for the good of others.

INDEX

ABOUT THE AUTHOR

Graham Cochrane is a business coach, YouTuber, and host of *The Graham Cochrane Show* podcast where each week he teaches people how to grow their online business, work less, and live and give more to the things and people they care about. As a lifelong musician and audio engineer, Graham founded his first online business, the Recording Revolution, in 2009 during the Great Recession as a blog and YouTube channel dedicated to teaching musicians how to record professional-sounding music at home on a budget. The Recording Revolution has grown to become a million-dollar-a-year business, with more than 600,000 subscribers tuning in from every single country in the world, and requires less than 5 hours of work per week.

In 2018, Graham launched GrahamCochrane.com as a resource dedicated to helping people build online income streams around their knowledge, passions, and skills. He has been featured in the *Huffington Post*, Yahoo!, and *Business Insider*. Through his podcast and YouTube channel, Graham delivers practical and relatable online business-building content each and every week.

He lives in Tampa, Florida, with his wife, Shay, and daughters, Chloe and Vera.

LAUNCH YOUR ONLINE BUSINESS IN THE NEXT 30 DAYS

Ready to take what you've learned in this book and launch your own income stream in the next 30 days? Then I have a bonus gift for you!

Inside the *30 Day Online Income Jumpstart Guide*, you'll discover:

- A 4-week step-by-step plan to go from no audience to earning income
- How to build an audience online with simple free tools
- How to co-create your first digital product with your audience

Also as a bonus, you'll receive an exclusive 45-minute training video called *The $1K Course Blueprint* to help you make your first $1000 as quickly as possible!

Go to GrahamCochrane.com/30daybonus to get started →